The World Wide Web

Beneath the surf

Mark Handley & Jon Crowcroft
University College London

UCL
PRESS

First published in 1995 by UCL Press

UCL Press Limited
University College London
Gower Street
London WC1E 6BT

The name of University College London (UCL) is a registered trade mark
used by UCL Press with the consent of the owner.

British Library Cataloguing in Publication Data
A catalogue record for this book is available from the British Library.

Library of Congress Cataloging-in-Publication Data are available

ISBN: 1-85728-435-6 PB

Typeset in Sabon and Gill Sans
Printed and bound by
Page Bros (Norwich), England.

Contents

Preface

The World Wide Web, the first global networked information service that is truly friendly, is probably the fastest growing technological phenomenon in the history of the human race (except maybe gambling). Recent statistics on the number of active Web sites available on the Internet are as follows:

Jun 93	130
Oct 93	212
Dec 93	623
Jun 94	3100
Jan 95	15768

Even more impressive has been the range of uses people have put the Web to. There are simple online versions of information that we are used to getting through paper, such as university prospectuses, and train and TV programme timetables, but there are also Cardiff's Movie Database, an online catalogue of excerpts of CDs from a record company, a national newspaper (quite a few now), a huge database of images of a dissected human body. There are also guides, tutorials, libraries, businesses and so on.

If you could buy shares in this phenomenon, no-one would invest in anything else! This outpaces the growth of the Internet (the underlying transmission networks), which is merely growing at about 7 per cent per month, and the Internet is often cited as generating several billion dollars worth of business a year.

This book is about how the World Wide Web (WWW) works. It is not another guide to what information there is out there, as that would be a waste of paper, being obsolete before it was printed. It is not about where to "surf", but about what happens "beneath the surf".

This book is aimed at information users and providers who wish to have a better idea about what is going on *under the bonnet*, e.g. publishers, librarians, students, IT managers at businesses, and just about anyone who can read a manual and set up a PC or Mac to run a client, or can use an editor to create and store pages. Typically, readers will either not yet have Internet access or may just be starting up. For the more experienced, a great deal of this material is available on the net in any case, and at no cost except the time to find it! Soon people will learn to use all of this at school, and will have WWW/ Internet access from their TV-top terminal, but not soon enough – hence this book. In fact, you do not need any network access at all to use WWW to organize your information, nor do you have to be connected to the Internet to use WWW to provide remote information access within your organization if you have a private network. However, the additional value of access to and from other organizations via the Internet is widely acknowledged.

By the time you have finished reading this book you should be able to start up a server on a Unix or Mac platform. You will have pointers, which this technology then makes it easy to follow, to where to find more information. We reference many other information services, and mention other client and server implementations. However, space and time preclude these mentions being more than cursory or the list being more than partial. We also believe in saving trees.

Outline/organization

The book is divided into ten chapters, and these can be read in four stages. In the first three chapters, we look at the technology of the network and at information servers and then specifically introduce the World Wide Web. In the next two chapters, we look in some technical detail at World Wide Web clients and servers. After this, we spend two chapters looking at some real-world WWW servers and see how people have used them to provide information to an academic community, to entertainment seekers and to a business community. In each we attempt to portray elements of style, both for documents within the Web, and for structure across the Web. The next chapter is technical detail on servers, exploring their components, configuration and usage, including caching and security. Finally, we survey some of the problems, and the future directions in which the WWW is heading.

In the appendices, we include information on the formal definition of some components of the WWW, some pointers to other Internet resource guides, and some notes on how to get connected and a few very simple good WWW places to go surfing. We do not list lots of favourite cyber-tourist resorts as virtual fashions and weather change too rapidly for a book to be a valid medium to store that kind of information.

The technology in the World Wide Web is evolving incredibly rapidly. It is certain that some descriptions in this book of features or bugs will be out of date by the time it is printed. This is inevitable with this technology. We hope that our fairly modest crystal ball gazing will not go awry (as Azimov's fictional techno-prophet Hari Seldon's did in the second of the Foundation series books), but that, too, is as inevitable as the further success of the WWW itself.

Typographic conventions

In any book with technical content, especially where computers are concerned, it is important to have clear typographic conventions. Where we show literally in the text what a computer has output, it will usually be in a typewriter font. In all cases this has been captured from a terminal. Where output is graphical, it is actually captured from the screen.

Disclaimer

The technology in the Web, as with the Internet itself, is a co-operative effort, and as such it is often hard to give credit to all where due. Our thanks to all for such a marvel. Our apologies to unsung heroes.

Acknowledgements

Thanks are due to the regular suspects and *The Daily Telegraph*, the BBC and Carl Phillips Yachting for permission to use their material.

We would also like to thank Nikos Drakos from the Computer Based Learning Unit, University of Leeds, the Students at UCL CS (guinea pigs), Andrew Carrick at UCL Press, Graeme Wood from EUCS, Nigel Edwards from Hewlett-Packard and ANSA, James E. [Jed] Donnelley from LLNL, Clifford Rosney, Paul Harrington, Martin Hamilton of Loughborough University, Dept of Computer Studies, Richard Stevens and Chris Clack for detailed feedback on early manuscripts.

Chapter 1
The Information Highstreet – introduction

The Internet is the Information Superhighway; it has become a cliché to say so. However, before embarking on a drive around the World Wide Web (WWW), it is important to understand how the roads themselves work (and to understand who pays road tax).

The Internet is undergoing a stormy adolescence as it moves from being a playground for academics into a commercial service. With more than 50 per cent of the network being commercially provided, and more than 50 per cent of the subscribers being businesses, the Internet is now a very different place from what it was in the 1980s. Growth has occurred most sharply in Europe, and in the commercial sector in the past two years. This has led to the critical problem of dealing with change. And change must be dealt with. Along with routing and addressing, there is also a crisis in security (or lack of it) and in accountability. These factors have led to the most interesting debate in the history of communications, as political, economic and technical concerns become inextricably intertwined.

There are two aspects of the technology. The first is host software (applications and support), which forms what one might call the "Information Services". The second is network support, which is the access and transfer technology used to move the information around.

First, a brief history of the Internet will give some clues as to its success, and will give some context to understanding how WWW works and fits together with the rest of the Information Highstreet.

Internet history

The Internet started life as a report written by the Rand Corporation for the US government in the 1960s. This outlined the very modern view of information supplanting material goods as the commodity of the coming century.

The US government agency ARPA, the Advanced Research Project Agency, invested several billion dollars in developing "packet switching networks" through the early 1970s. Initially, the customer for these was the US Department of Defense. However, many of the researchers contracted to carry out the work were academics, who became enamoured of the test systems they built. Initially, the research network was called the ARPANET, later renamed the Internet.

By the very early 1980s, two other important pieces of technology had been developed. First, the workstation/server system was starting to emerge as the way to provide cost effective computing to the desktop. Secondly, the Ethernet local area network was broadly accepted as the way of providing communications between the desktop and server computers in the same organization. The same researchers used all these systems for computing, local and national (US) communications.

A curious footnote to this history was that the US government funded most of the initial implementations of the Internet technology on the basis that it would be made freely available to others. This was in direct contrast to the expensive communications solutions provided by computing and telecommunications companies that conformed to international standards promulgated by the ITU (International Telecommunications Union) and ISO (International Standards Organization).

By the late 1980s, a large proportion of universities and research laboratories in Europe and the USA had access to the Internet through largely government-subsidized network links leased from the public network operators. However, this changed rapidly, so that now many Internet connections are paid for directly by subscribing organizations.

On the standards front, it became obvious that people were "voting with their feet", but that the Internet protocols (the communications languages used to glue all this together) needed to have a more acceptable status. Hence, the Internet Society, an international not-for-profit professional body formed to allow individuals, government agencies and companies to have a direct say in the direction that the protocols and the technology could move, was formed.

This is now very much the state we are in today and, except for one other thing, would not really explain the recent massive growth in interest in the Internet. That one thing is the World Wide Web, of which more in a moment.

Hosts, networks and routers

The components that make up the Internet are threefold, as illustrated in Figure 1.1. First, there are hosts, the workstations, PCs, servers, and mainframes on which we run our applications. Then there are networks, the local area

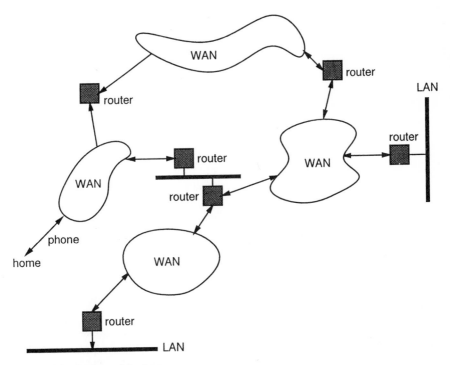

Figure 1.1   A piece of the Internet.

networks (Ethernets), point-to-point leased lines, dial-up (telephone, ISDN, X25) links, that carry traffic between one computer and another, and finally there are routers. These glue together all the different network technologies to provide a ubiquitous service to deliver packets (a packet is a small unit of data convenient for computers to bundle up data for sending and receiving). Routers are usually just special purpose computers that are good at talking to network links. Some people use general purpose machines as low performance (low cost) routers, e.g. PCs or Unix boxes with multiple local area network (LAN) cards or serial line cards or modems.

Names, addresses and routes

Every computer (host or router) in a well run part of the Internet has a name. The name is usually given to a device by its owner. Internet names are actually hierarchical, and look rather like postal addresses. Jon's computer's name is waffle.cs.ucl.ac.uk. We allocated it the name "waffle". The department we work in called itself "CS". The university it is in called itself "UCL". The academic community called themselves "ac", and the Americans called us the "UK". The name tells me what something is *organizationally*. The Internet calls this the Domain Name System. Names in this system are "case insensitive", which means that it makes no difference whether you give them in capitals or not.

Everything in any part of the Internet that needs to be reached must have an address. The address tells the computers in the Internet (hosts and routers) where something is topologically. Thus the address is also hierarchical. My computer's address is 128.16.8.88. We asked the IANA (Internet Assigned Numbers Authority) for a network number. We were given the number 128.16.x.y. We could fill in the x and y how we liked, to number the computers on our network. We divided our computers into groups on different LAN segments, and numbered the segments 1–256 (x), and then the hosts 1–256 (y) on each segment. When your organization asks for a number for its net, it will be asked how many computers it has, and assigned a network number big enough to accommodate that number of computers. Nowadays, if you have a large network, you will be given a number of numbers. The task of allocating numbers to sites in the Internet has now become so vast that it is delegated to a number of organizations around the world – ask your Internet provider where they get the numbers from if you are interested.

Everything in the Internet must be reachable. The route to a host will traverse one or more networks. The easiest way to picture a route is by thinking of how a letter gets to a friend in a foreign country. You post the letter in a postbox. It is picked up by a postman (LAN), and taken to a sorting office (router). There, the sorter looks at the address, sees that the letter is for another country and sends it to the sorting office for international mail, where a similar procedure is carried out. And so on, until the letter gets to its destination. If the letter was for the same "network" then it would immediately be delivered locally. Notice the fact that each router (sorting office) does not have to know all the details about everywhere, just about the next hop to make. Notice also that the routers (sorting offices) have to consult tables of where to go next (e.g. international sorting office). Routers chatter to each other all the time figuring out the best (or even just usable) routes to places.

The way to picture this is to imagine a road system with a person who is working for the Road Observance Brigade standing at every intersection. This person (Rob) reads the names of the roads meeting at the intersection, and writes them down on a card, with the number 0 after each name. Every few minutes, Rob holds up the card to any neighbour standing down the road at the next intersection. If the neighbour is doing the same, Rob writes down their list, but adds 1 to each number read off the other card. After a while, Rob is now telling people about the neighbours' roads several intersections away. Of course, Rob may get the same name from two different neighbours, i.e. two routes to a road. He then crosses out the one with the larger number.

Performance

The Internet today moves packets around without due regard to any special priorities. The speed a packet goes, once it starts to be transmitted, is the speed of the wire (LAN, point-to-point link, dial up or what have you) on the next hop. We illustrate the range of communication technology speeds in Figure 1.2. However, if there are a lot of users, packets get held up inside routers (like letters in sorting offices at Christmas). Because the Internet is designed to be interactive, rather than the slow turnaround of mail (even electronic mail), routers generally do not hang on to packets for very long. Instead, they just "drop them on the floor" when things get too busy.

This then means that hosts have to deal with a network that loses packets. Hosts generally have conversations that last a little longer than a single packet – at the least, a packet in each direction, but usually several in each direction.

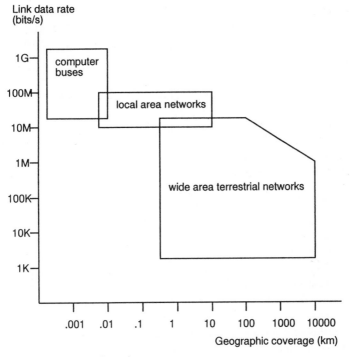

Figure 1.2   Range of network performance.

In fact, it is worse than that. The network can automatically decide to change the routes it is using because of a problem somewhere. Then it is possible for a new route to appear that is better. Suddenly, all packets will follow the new route. However, if there were already some packets half way along the old route, they may get there after some of the later packets (a bit like people driving to a party and some smart late driver taking a short cut and overtaking those who started earlier).

So a host has to be prepared to put up with out of order packets, as well as lost packets.

Protocols

All this communication is done using standard "languages" to exchange blocks of data in packets, simply by putting "envelopes" or wrappers called "headers" around the packet. We try to illustrate how and why this is so in Figure 1.3.

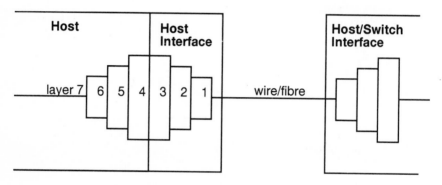

Figure 1.3   Protocol "layering".

The work of routing and addressing is done by the Internet Protocol (IP) and the work of host communications by the Transmission Control Protocol (TCP). TCP/IP is often used as the name for the Internet protocols, including some of the higher level information services that this book is mainly about. TCP does all the work to solve the problems of packet loss, corruption and re-ordering that the IP layer may have introduced through a number of *end to end* reliability and error recovery mechanisms. If you like, you can think of IP as a bucket brigade and TCP as drainpipe.

So if we want to send a block of data, we put a TCP header on it to protect it from wayward network events and then we put an IP header on it to get it routed to the right place. There are many different protocols in the world, and we show some of them in all their gory glory in Figure 1.4.

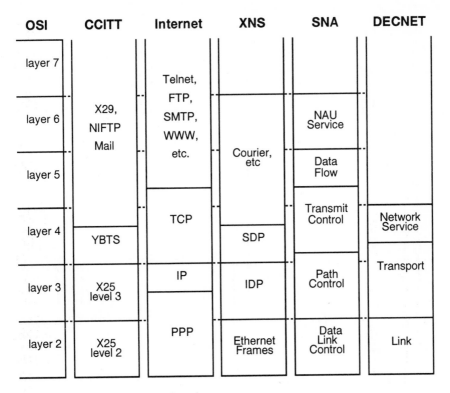

Figure 1.4   Comparing protocol stacks.

Host and applications

The emergence of some simple APIs (application programming interfaces) and
GUIs (graphical user interfaces) has led to the rapid growth of new user-
friendly applications in the Internet. Information services provided by archive
and Web servers are accessible through WWW and Mosaic, Archie and Prospero, Gopher, and WAIS and Z39.50.

In Figure 1.5, we can see a screen dump of a workstation running Mosaic,
the most popular client program for accessing the Web Servers around the
world. In this picture, we can see a window showing a map of the UK and two
other pictures, both photographs in GIF (graphics interchange format). At the
top right is a picture of UCL, where we work. At the lower right is a satellite
image stored on Edinburgh University Computing Service's Web server every
hour, from a live satellite weather feed, which comes from one of the many
weather satellites that send out unencrypted images periodically over the
ether. Many sites simply point a satellite dish in the right direction and soak up
the data for later dissemination on the terrestrial Internet.

7

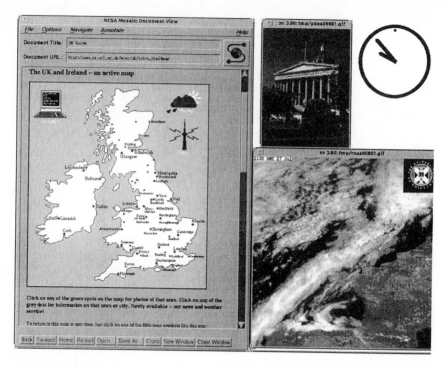

Figure 1.5   Spot on surf.

The value of the service is now clearly becoming the value of the informa-tion, rather than the communications channel. This means that some mecha-nism for charging and auditing access to information is a new requirement. This must be a secure mechanism to assure people that charges (or audit trails) are correct.

In Figure 1.6, we can see a screen dump with four applications running. On the right is a Gopher client, the bottom left is Archie, the top centre is WAIS and the bottom centre is FTP. Gopher allows us to access information through a menu/browsing system. In this example, you can see a list of subjects that we can browse. Archie allows us to search for software or documents in some of the large archive server repositories. In this example, we have retrieved a list of sites that have a document introducing TCP/IP. This and other services are explained further in Chapter 2. The Wide Area Information Service (WAIS) allows servers to build searchable indexes of many types of documents. In this example, we have retrieved a list of documents about acid rain from a set of servers that hold information about ecology. From all of these interfaces, hav-ing found a piece of information, we can retrieve it, print it or mail it to other people.

New end-systems such as laptops and palmtops are leading to the require-

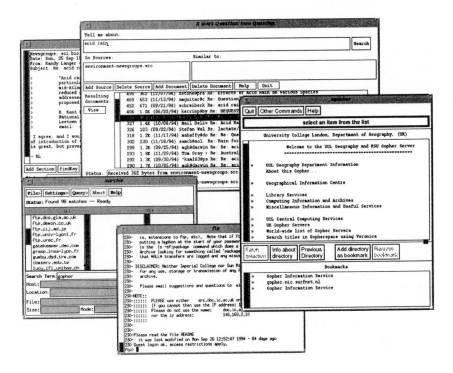

Figure 1.6   Information servers galore.

ment for access to home systems by travellers. This leads to a new requirement for mobile communications support in the Internet, both while people are travelling and when they arrive at a new site.

Most new systems have the power to handle sound and vision, as well as text and graphics. This multimedia requirement leads to the need for integrated services in the network, in order to support the delay-intolerant applications that are emerging from the research and development world into products.

The vast number of systems attaching to the Internet leads to whole new problems in management. We foresee a time when every home will have many networkable devices (VCRs, heating/lighting, surveillance and so on). WWW is just the start of this revolution.

Network functionality

The growth of the Internet is remarkable. It is sustaining an exponential increase in end systems at 100 per cent per annum, although this is a cautious estimate based on the host count made by Mark Lotter of DNS-registered hosts. The true number is much higher than this, but by how much, no-one can accurately say. This has led the community to start to worry about the current limits, and consider a next generation Internet protocol, the basic glue that holds the whole system together. Studying this is a good guide to how the Internet works so well today.

Internet futures

First, we must ask ourselves whether "more is better". Is it advisable to permit the increase to go on? The answer must be yes, since the market has chosen this technology, but we must solve the scaling problems first and foremost.

Another interesting question to ask ourselves is: What were the original Internet requirements? The Internet evolved out of a defence experiment, with special requirements for robustness above all else. This has led to the possibility of running a severely under-engineered network and still getting useful service from it. We need to persuade the public network operators to provide a properly engineered Internet service (somewhat like the latest NSFNet service in the USA). This is covered in more detail in Chapter 10. Luckily, the community, the Internet Engineering Task Force (IETF), has this attitude: better leads to more anyhow!

The next generation of the Internet is going to be based on a protocol called the Simple Internet Protocol Plus, now known as IP6, using a variety of mechanisms to improve all the services above. (It will have version number 6, as opposed to 5 which is one more than the current IP version, as an experimental real-time protocol called ST is using 5.)

The next generation Internet and its competitors

The Internet is not without its competitors in the information haulage business. The main two technologies that are emerging as either competitive or complementary are ATM/Broadband ISDN and "video-on-demand".

The telecommunications companies have developed ATM/Broadband ISDN (B-ISDN), a next generation architecture for their backbone networks, to carry telephony, and all the other services as well. There is also a move to make this a LAN service, and thus a replacement for the Internet. Whether this latter move succeeds remains to be seen.

As we explained above, the Internet is starting to experiment with audio and video. However, there is also a move afoot to provide video-on-demand services by consortia of cable TV and telecommunications companies. Since this can be done using existing telephony cabling, it is clearly a low-cost approach to delivery of entertainment quality video. This is complementary to the Internet, and indeed, in some experimental services, the Internet is used to carry requests to video-on-demand servers. It is also possible to use the inbound path to the home as a carrier for higher-bandwidth Internet traffic when the video traffic is quieter.

Policies

The Internet abounds with policies. There are policies on name allocation, policies on address allocation and policies on routes. There are also policies on use of network resources (bandwidth), since bandwidth is the most precious resource, and costs money. Your Internet provider will make you aware of policies relevant to your business. A common misunderstanding about the Internet is the belief that you cannot use it for commercial traffic. This is not the case at all. What is the case is that some parts of the Internet, e.g. the academic parts, are part of the infrastructure of government or state organizations and are typically paid for that use, either on a per usage basis or simply for, say, year round access. Sometimes the rates negotiated for a large organization's collective access are specifically on the basis that it does not sell usage on. In times gone past, commercial use was seen as potentially undermining the quality of such funded parts of the network, or as undermining the justification for state subsidy for access to the net for the agencies concerned.

There is still a fiery debate raging about charging policies and mechanisms. The prevailing technical wind is behind the idea of keeping to a minimum usage-based charging, e.g. connect time or number of packets sent, perhaps only charging for a premium service when the network is overloaded/congested. However, the old public network operator view, that more income is made by charging all the time, is hovering in the wings, despite the evidence that it costs a huge percentage of profit to collect such charges and that it discourages new users. We believe that charging in proportion to the value of data delivered from information services is a far more valid approach, and that the networks really will become much like the roads in terms of cost recovery.

There is also the social phenomenon that has arisen called *Netiquette*, which includes a whole range of unwritten rules about what is and what is not acceptable use and behaviour "on the net". Unsolicited posting of advertising is certainly regarded as *verboten*. On the other hand, appropriate use of non-invasive advertising (bulletin boards or WWW pages for the express purpose thereof) is certainly not frowned on.

Chapter 2

Information – are you being served?

We are familiar with ways to get information in the non-network world. We can go to a library or buy a book in a bookshop. We can telephone companies or individuals by looking up their names in a phonebook. We can sit around and watch TV or listen to the radio. In the networked world, there are a number of ways of carrying out the same kinds of activities, using programs that run on a PC or workstation to access information servers in the network that hopefully hold the knowledge we seek.

Information on the net used to be about as hard to retrieve as computers were to use. Nowadays retrieval is usually fairly easy if you can find the information. First you have to know what kind of server holds it (this is rather like knowing whether a written item is in a reference book, a novel, a magazine, newspaper or shopping list). We illustrate in Figure 2.1 the array of available information servers as seen from a very high level view of layered services.

Different kinds of information services have different models of use and different ways they hold information. Almost all fit into the "client/server" model that has become widespread in distributed computing. Client/server communication is quite easy to understand in terms of roles and is very closely analogous to what happens in a shopping situation. An assistant in a shop awaits a customer. The assistant does not know in advance which customer might arrive (or even how many – the store manager is supposed to make sure that enough assistants are employed to just about cope with the maximum number of shoppers arriving at any one time). A server on the network is typically a dedicated computer that runs a program also called the server. This awaits requests from the network, according to some specified protocol, and serves them, one or more at a time, without regard for whom they come from.

There are a variety of refinements of this model, such as requiring authentication or registration with the server before other kinds of transactions can be undertaken, but almost all the basic systems on the Internet now work like this.

We can categorize information servers along a number of different axes:

- **Synchronous versus asynchronous** Synchronous servers respond as you

Users

Netscape, Mosaic, Netfind, Cello	Browser/Search applications

URL, URN, DNS	Hyperlink management
CGI	

WAIS, Archie, Gopher, etc.	Search & Index tools

Email, Telnet, FTP, HTTP	Data retrieval tools

TCP/IP
SLIP/PPP
Information stores and high streets

Figure 2.1   The whole cornucopia of cyberspace.

type/click at your computer. Asynchronous ones save up their answers and return them some time later. Sometimes, your system will actually not even send the request for information to the server until you have finished composing the whole thing, or even later, to save time (and possibly money, since night-time network access may be cheaper and/or faster).

- **Browsable versus searchable**   Some servers allow you to move from one piece of information to another. Typically, the managers/keepers have structured the information with links, or else the information is hierarchical (like most large organizations' job structures or payrolls). Other servers allow you to search for particular items by giving keywords. Usually, this means that the managers of the information have created indexes, although sometimes it just means that the server is running on a very fast computer that can search all through the data. This latter approach is becoming increasing impossible as the quantity of information kept online grows to massive proportions.

- **Distributed versus replicated**   Some information servers hold only the information entered at their site, and maybe have links for the user to follow to other servers at other sites. Other systems copy the information around at quiet times, so that all servers are replicas of each other. In the latter case this means that it does not matter which server you access, so you may as well go for the nearest or cheapest (likely to be both).

13

Transport protocols

The Internet provides a way to get packets (convenient units of data for computers and routers) from any host computer to one or more other host computers. However, the network protocols make no guarantees about delivering a packet. In fact, a packet may get lost, may arrive after others sent later or may be distorted. A packet may even arrive that simply was not sent.

To counter this, host computers incorporate transport protocols, which not only use the Internet to carry the application information around, but also send a variety of other information to provide checking and correction or recovery from such errors.

There is a spectrum of complexity in transport protocols, depending on the application requirements. The three representative ones are:

- **User Datagram Protocol (UDP)** UDP is a "send and forget" protocol. It provides just enough control information at the start of each packet to tell what application is running and to check if the packet was distorted on route. UDP is typically used by applications that have no requirement for an answer and do not really care if the message is received. A typical example of this might be a server that announces the time on the network, unsolicited.

- **Reliable Data Protocol (RDP)** RDP is a generic name for a collection of protocols – the most relevant here is the one used by Prospero (see later). RDP type protocols are similar to TCP, but with reduced complexity at the start and end of a conversation and with good support for sequences of exchanges of chunks of data, often known as remote procedure calls or sometimes incorrectly called transactions.

- **Transmission Control Protocol (TCP)** TCP is the protocol module that provides reliability and safety. TCP is designed to cope with the whole gamut of network failures and adapts elegantly to the available resources in the network. It even tries to be fair to all users.

Transport interfaces

The application programming interfaces to the above protocols also vary. TCP resembles a pipe: at either end you feed in bytes, and at the other end the same bytes come out. UDP resembles a bucket. You pile your bytes in at one end, pass the bucket, and the other end gets the bucket load of bytes (or not, if the network loses them). RDPs are in between. Typically, they provide a bucket-style interface, but a sequence of buckets alternating in direction.

The most common programming interface to all these protocols is called sockets, or winsock on DOS machines. Some Unix boxes also provide an interface called streams.

Ports

All of these protocols make use of an idea called "ports". The Internet normally only provides one address for a computer (or one for each of its network attachments at least). If you want to carry on more than one conversation between two computers, you need extra detailed addressing (like a little extra set of in and out trays). At the same time, you want to distinguish different kinds of conversation, e.g. terminal access from file transfer. This is achieved by reserving a number of port numbers. Then all transport protocol packets carry the port number of the application in the server/destination field, as well as some uniquely chosen port number for this particular conversation in the source/client field, when going from the client to the server, and vice versa in the other direction. Well known ports are listed in the Assigned Numbers RFC. (An RFC is a request for comments, and is part of the standardization process of the Internet Engineering Task Force.) We say that a server (or "daemon") runs on port "so and so".

Remote Procedure Call (RPC)

Some applications, e.g. WWW, use a wrapper for the transport protocol to make it easier (more natural) to use for application programmers, who may not be used to networks. This is called Remote Procedure Call, or RPC. RPC makes a procedure in a program running as a server on the network look as though it is available to any other program as a client on another machine. The idea came from Xerox in the late 1970s, and is very cute: when you call a procedure in any programming language like C, C++, Pascal etc., you wrap up a bunch of data in some parameters and then the program jumps to the procedure. When the procedure is finished, it wraps up any results, and jumps back.

So, you have a Remote Procedure Call if the parameters are put into a packet for the call and sent to the right server; the server does its work, puts the results into another packet and returns it to the calling client. The piece of code between the program and the transport protocol that does this is called a stub and can be automatically built by a smart compiler.

There are only a couple more tricks required:

- **Binding** The client has to find the right server.

- **Data formats** The client and server may be different kinds of machines – say a Pentium and a Sparc server. Their ideas of format for even the simplest thing, say an integer variable, may be very different. So the "wrapping up" or stub processing stage must include converting formats to some network-agreed standard. This is typically called an External Data Representation protocol.

Sockets

Sockets are an API to communications that make a remote program look as though it is a file, but a file that you can write things to and read different things back from. This means that many of the programs on DOS and Unix systems that operate on local files can be changed to use a stream or datagram socket and work, very simply, to a remote system.

Telnet

Telnet provides remote terminal access between PCs and workstations and server. It uses a TCP connection to port 23 to carry ASCII text typed by the user to the remote computer, and output from the application on the remote computer back to the user.

File Transfer Protocol (FTP)

The original information service was called FTP (File Transfer Protocol). This is probably the world's least friendly information service. It operates at the level of machine–machine communication, and is used by more modern client programs just as a way of getting something from a server. However, it is still used by people as a sort of lowest-common-denominator means of access to a file on a remote computer. The following shows a printout of a real FTP session:

```
ftp bells
Connected to bells.cs.ucl.ac.uk.
220 bells.cs.ucl.ac.uk FTP server (SunOS 4.0) ready.
Name (bells:jon): anonymous
331 Guest login ok, send ident as password.
Password:
230 Guest login ok, access restrictions apply.
ftp> cd darpa
250 CWD command successful.
ftp> ls
200 PORT command successful.
150 ASCII data connection for /bin/ls (128.16.8.88,1284) (0 bytes).
tcpdump.tar.Z
ttcp.c.Z
226 ASCII Transfer complete.
1485 bytes received in 0.25 seconds (5.8 Kbytes/s)
ftp> bin
```

```
200 Type set to I.
ftp> get ttcp.c.Z
200 PORT command successful.
150 Binary data connection for ttcp.c.Z
(128.16.8.88.1285) (6710 bytes).
226 Binary Transfer complete.
local: ttcp.c.Z remote: ttcp.c.Z
6710 bytes received in 0.025 seconds (2.6e+02 Kbytes/s)
ftp> close
221 Goodbye.
ftp> quit
```

Internet FTP is interactive or synchronous, which means that you formulate your commands as you type at the terminal. FTP maintains a control connection between the client and server, and sends commands over this in ASCII, or ordinary text. When data is going to move, the client and server open a data connection. The data connection can keep going whilst the user issues further commands.

There are three categories of FTP commands on the control channel:

- **Access Control**   User, Passwd, Account, CWD, CDUP, QUIT;

- **Transfer Parameters**   Type, Structure, Mode;

- **File Service Commands**   Retrieve, Store, Append, etc.

Basically, users are asked to type a set of commands to access a file on a remote computer that may well resemble those they might type on accessing a file on the local computer. The additional information required includes: the name of the remote computer; account information for permission to access the remote computer; and differences in the way files are kept remotely and locally. None of these things is very friendly to the non-computer user.

A common technique for sharing information freely using FTP is to provide an anonymous account that people can use to access public files on an FTP server. When challenged to login, users give the name anonymous and, when asked for a password, they simply reply with their email address (or name, or sometimes, just the word guest).

The two most useful things in FTP are the ability to get a listing of files in a directory on a remote server and the ability to retrieve multiple files by wildcard matching of file names. The least useful things about FTP are that you have to know something about the name of the file you are seeking, as well as where it is; you also need to understand that there is not necessarily any connection between that name and what is in the file.

Electronic mail and info-servers

Electronic mail, or email, is either the saviour of modern society, and trees, or the devil on the icing on the cake of technocracy. Electronic mail, at its simplest, is a replacement for paper letters ("snail" mail) or for facsimile/fax. Sending email is easy, if you know the address of the person you want to get it to. You type in the message using whatever facility you are familiar with, and then submit it to the mail system (put it in the postmaster's postbag). Then a series of automatic systems (message handlers) will sort it and carry it to the destination, just as post offices and sorting offices do with paper mail.

A message one of us received recently is:

```
Return-Path: <72633.1504@compuserve.com>
Received: from arl-img-2.compuserve.com by
bells.cs.ucl.ac.uk
    with Internet SMTP
    id VAA16571; Sun, 21 Aug 1994 21:23:01 -0400
Date: 21 Aug 94 21:21:24 EDT
From: Neil Belcher <72633.1504@compuserve.com>
To: MATHEW B BELCHER <74537.1464@compuserve.com>
Cc: Declan McKeever <d.mckeever@cgnet.com>,
    Johnny & Noreen <J.Crowcroft@cs.ucl.ac.uk>,
    CLIFFORD ROSNEY <100333.1560@compuserve.com>
Subject: Tornado Hits Dryden
Message-ID: <940822012123_72633.1504_DHL67-1@CompuServe.COM>

Hey, we got hit by a pretty nasty "Tornado" this morning -
```

The protocol used for electronic mail in the Internet is called the Simple Mail Transfer Protocol or SMTP. The model is of message handling systems and user agents all talking to each other. Both use same protocol. The user program invokes SMTP to send to a receiver.

The receiver may be a mail relay or an actual recipient system.

A SMTP mail address look like this:

```
J.Crowcroft@cs.ucl.ac.uk
```

and the general form of such an address is:

```
User@Domain
```

The domain is as defined in the Domain Name System (DNS) for the host implementing SMTP. The DNS name is translated to an IP address. The sending system merely opens a TCP connection to the site and then talks the SMTP protocol. SMTP control is ASCII (text) based commands and responses over the TCP connection.

After the sender connects, commands include:

```
HELO
MAIL FROM: reverse path
RECPT TO: forward path
DATA
lines of message
<CRLF>.<CRLF>
QUIT
```

(Try "telnet machine smtp". In fact, for many information services, the application search or browse protocol is text based and can be driven by a human typing, albeit rather obscure commands, rather than a client GUI program. Try this with WWW: telnet www.cs.ucl.ac.uk 80. See later chapters for what to type next and what comes back.)

The message "body" includes fields in the same way as an inter-office memo:

```
From: Mark Handley <M.Handley@cs.ucl.ac.uk>
To: J.Crowcroft@cs.ucl.ac.uk
Subject: Re: Did you get "Re: Mbone Documentation" ?
In-reply-to: Your message of "02 Jun 94 17:44:48 BST."
Date: Thu, 02 Jun 94 17:56:28 +0100
Sender: M.Handley@cs.ucl.ac.uk
```

The site you connect to may be a relay. Relays are configured by hand, with routing tables, in a way exactly analogous to Post Office sorting offices. Systems often use default entries to mail out of a large site.

The receiving system maybe an info-server. This is a special mail system that delivers messages to a server program rather than a human or a mailbox. This program will understand some simple set of commands in the message. Often these are a subset of file access commands from FTP. Thus a user need only be familiar with email, rather than the whole gamut of possible obscure commands to an FTP system, to be able to send or retrieve documents from a server.

The SMTP protocol that carries electronic mail in the Internet is restricted to seven-bit clean ASCII, i.e. printable characters only. Also the body of an RFC 822 compliant message has no structure. (RFC 822 is the basic standard for Internet electronic mail.) However, both of these shortcomings are removed by the MIME standard, which is described in the next chapter, along with WWW, in some detail.

A third shortcoming of Internet mail is the lack of security mechanisms (privacy, authenticity, integrity, non-repudiation, etc.) that are required if we wish to use email on a legal (say contractual) basis. These are fixed in the Privacy

19

Enhanced Mail standard, but export controls between some countries and legal restrictions on private or corporate use of encryption in others are hindering the deployment of this technology.

Mail lists

Some mail system managers use info-servers to maintain mail lists. Mail lists are ways of sending a message at one go to groups of people possessing a common interest or purpose. They resemble, but are completely different in implementation from, bulletin boards, of which more below. Mail lists are very useful when used with discrimination. On the other hand, because it is as easy to send to a list as to an individual, sometimes users propagate junk mail to large groups of people. The most common typical piece of junk mail is to do with list management (e.g. "please add me to this list" or "please remove me from this list", which should be directed to list managers, usually as "*listname-request*"), but other human errors include sending irrelevant or offensive information. Some (some might say paranoid) sites restrict list usage strictly to internal inter-office memos.

List maintenance is carried out in a centralized way. At a mail-system site, a user creates a list name and sets up the contents, the list of each member's personal email address (typically by putting them in a file). Then users can send to the list by sending to the list name at the central server machine.

There are a couple of other features of lists worth mentioning. Lists can be moderated, where material is "censored" by a list maintainer or moderator before being circulated. Many lists also provide digests, terms of reference, FAQs (frequently asked questions) and so forth periodically to those on the list, to pre-empt repetition of discussions, and to reduce traffic.

Bulletin boards

Online bulletin boards (bboards) are analogous to the pinboards we are all used to from offices, schools and so on. The difference between a bboard and a mail list is fundamental: Mail arrives in an individual's mailbox, and the individual's attention is drawn to it, while bulletins arrive on a bboard and users decide whether or when they want to read that bboard, if at all.

Less fundamental is the protocol. A bulletin board is effectively a single mailbox. Thus the overhead of delivery in terms of computer storage is much lower for a bboard than for a mail list.

Archie

Archive servers appeared in the mid 1980s. Initially, they were a logical extension of FTP servers. They provide indexed repositories of files for retrieval through a simple protocol called Prospero.

Archive servers had been in place manually for some time, simply as well maintained FTP servers. The first attempt at automating co-ordination was to use a simple protocol. This involved periodically exchanging a recursive directory listing of all the files present on a given server with all other known servers. Thereafter, access to a given server for a file present on another could have two results: either the client could be redirected to the right server, or the current server could fetch it, and then return it to the client. These two approaches are called "referral" and "chaining" in some communities, or "iteration" and "recursion" in others. See below for further discussion of these ideas.

Archive servers are accessed using the Prospero protocol. Prospero is a third-generation remote object access protocol. (You can tell it is third generation as it talks about "objects" rather than files.) It runs on top of, i.e. encapsulated within, an RDP, which in turn is on top of UDP and IP.

The Prospero protocol is constructed out of commands in ASCII text, i.e. like FTP and SMTP, it is a human-readable protocol. Human-readable protocols are very easy to debug, and are highly portable and extensible.

Prospero is not entirely unlike FTP, except that it is slimmer and more abstract:

DIRECTORY	read or write a directory itself
LIST	List contents of a directory
GET-OBJECT-INFO	Retrieve attributes of an object
and so on . . .	

These then have responses, either the output from the command, or else Success, Forwarded, Error or Failure.

Whois/Finger/Netfind

Whois

Whois is one of the oldest and simplest information servers in the Internet. Whois allows you to look up someone's email address and other information that a user may be happy to give away, simply by knowing their name. Originally, whois was a purely central server run on the ARPANET for all managers/ contacts of networks attached to the ARPANET for the DCA (Defence Communications Agency).

Basically, a whois server runs on TCP port 43 and awaits simple command lines. In ASCII text these end with CRLF – "Carriage Return" (ASCII character 13) followed by "Line Feed" (ASCII character 10). The server simply looks up the command line or "name specification" in a file (perhaps using fuzzy or soundex matching) and responds, possibly with multiple matches. Whois is for keeping organization contact information:

```
whois -h ftp.ripe.net bates
person: Tony Bates
address: RIPE Network Coordination Centre (NCC)
address: PRIDE Project
address: Kruislaan 409
address: NL-1098 SJ Amsterdam
address: Netherlands
e-mail: Tony.Bates@ripe.net
nic-hdl: TB230
notify: Tony.Bates@ripe.net
changed: Tony.Bates@ripe.net 931230
source: RIPE
```

Note that each returned entry has a NIC (Network Information Center) handle, to distinguish it, i.e. act as a unique key.

Finger

The Finger protocol derives from RFC 742. A Finger server runs on UDP or TCP port 79. It expects either a null string, in which case a list of all people using the system is returned, or if a string is given, information available concerning that person is given (whether logged in or not).

Some people find the idea of Whois and Finger alarmingly insecure. One particular scare concerning security in the Internet was due to a simple, but extremely effective, gaping bug in the most widely used implementation of the Finger server, which may be why it scares some people. This bug has long since been fixed. Basically, the Finger daemon had storage for receiving a limited request/command, but could actually be handed a larger amount of information from the transport protocol. The extra information would overwrite the stack of the executing Finger server program. An ingenious hacker could exploit this by sending a Finger command carefully constructed with executable code that carried out his desired misdemeanour. The problem was exacerbated on many systems where the Finger server ran as a special privileged process (root), for no particular reason other than laziness of the designers of the default configuration. Thus the wily hacker gained access to arbitrary rights on the system.

The following is an example of the use of Finger:

```
finger jon@waffle.cs.ucl.ac.uk
[waffle.cs.ucl.ac.uk]
Login name: jon    In real life: Jon Crowcroft
Directory: /cs/research/jon/home/sol/jon    Shell: /bin/csh
On since Sep 12 09:31:03 on console
No unread mail
Project: charismatic phantasms
Plan:
my plan is to be spontaneous on demand
```

Netfind

Netfind is a smart combination of facilities designed to use a database gradually built up over time from network resources. The database that Netfind uses is a complex merge of information from a variety of sources:

```
netfind handley UCL Computer

Please select at most 3 of the following domains to search:
    0. ucl.ja.net (university of london computer centre, england,
                united kingdom)
    1. cc.ucl.ac.uk (computer center, university college london,
                england, united kingdom)
    2. cs.ucl.ac.uk (computer science department, university college
                london, england, united kingdom)
    3. ess.cs.ucl.ac.uk (university college london, department of
                computer science, london, england, united kingdom)
Enter selection (e.g., 2 0 1) -> 2
( 1) SMTP_Finger_Search: checking domain cs.ucl.ac.uk
( 1) do_connect: Finger service not available on host cs.ucl.ac.uk
            --> cannot do user lookup
---
Domain search completed. Proceeding to host search.
---
( 1) SMTP_Finger_Search: checking host eggs.cs.ucl.ac.uk
( 2) SMTP_Finger_Search: checking host salamanca.cs.ucl.ac.uk
( 3) SMTP_Finger_Search: checking host ns1.cs.ucl.ac.uk

SYSTEM: ns1.cs.ucl.ac.uk
    Login name: mhandley    In real life: Mark Handley
    Directory: /cs/research/mice/speedy/home/mhandley
```

```
Shell:/bin/csh
Last login Mon Aug 9, 1993 on ttyp0 from kant.cs.ucl.ac.u
No unread mail
Plan:
Ah, now I understand, the whole purpose of life is . . .
Floating exception - core dumped

Login name: mhandley     In real life: Mark Handley
Directory: /cs/research/mice/speedy/home/mhandley
              Shell: /etc/ucl/nologin
Last login Mon Aug 9, 1993 on ttyp0 from kant.cs.ucl.ac.
```

X.500 and Domain Name System

Domain Name System (DNS)

The Domain Name System is really designed as a network information service for internal use by tools rather than directly by users. However, the names it holds appear in location information currently used by many services and are also the basis for electronic mail routing.

The Domain Name System model is that all objects on the net have a name, and that the name should be that given by the people responsible for the object. However, this name is only part of the full way to specify the object. The fully distinguished name is part of a hierarchy of names. They are written as per postal "address", for example:

```
swan.computer-lab.cambridge.ac.uk
```

The "top level" is a country code (e.g. uk) or US Specific (e.g. com). Any organization owns its level and the names of the levels below. Any string is usable. Aliases are allowed – names are more friendly than addresses.

Any owner of a name space must run a server. The owning site must then inform sites at a "level" above, where its server is. At the same time, it tells its server where the level above is.

Applications (FTP, Mail, Telnet, Mosaic, etc.) use a library function to call the resolver. They give the resolver function a name and it sends a request to the local site DNS server. The DNS server responds with either:

- The answer (a) from its own tables or (b) from another server it asked on the user's behalf. This is called chaining, and is illustrated for a general directory service in Figure 2.2.

- A site that can answer. This is called referral, and is illustrated in Figure 2.3.

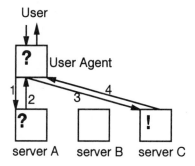

Figure 2.2   Chaining in servers.

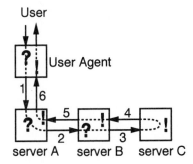

Figure 2.3   Referral in servers.

The Domain Name System holds general-purpose Resource Records (RRs). RRs are not restricted to describing just Name ↔ IP address, but can include: aliases, mail relay addresses, pointers to other DNS servers, start of authority, and network users and managers.

X.500

The X.500 system is not part of the Internet protocols, but is available on the Internet. X.500 is the ITU Directory Service (the ITU is International Telecommunications Union, the body that oversees all national telecom companies). This is a far more general information service than the DNS, and is targeted at providing White- and Yellow-page type information about organizations and people, as well as about computers. The *big* distinction between X.500 and DNS is that DNS is a simple lookup system, while the directory is searchable.

Other important differences include the fact that the directory has an update protocol and that it can be accessed securely (current work on DNS to add security/access control is not yet finished).

Otherwise, access to the directory and the structure of information in it (the Directory Information Tree) are typically quite similar to DNS. The general model is illustrated in Figure 2.4.

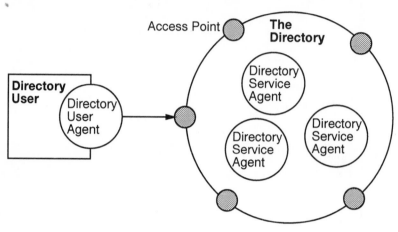

Figure 2.4   Directory services.

Wide Area Information Server (WAIS)

The Wide Area Information Server idea is based on a search model of information, rather than a browse one. Sites that run WAIS servers have created a collection of *indexed* data that can then be retrieved by searches on these indexes. The access protocol to WAIS servers is based on the standard developed for library searching by ANSI (American National Standards Institute) with the unlikely title Z39.50 (also known as the Information Retrieval Service and Protocol Standard).

WAIS has four parts (like most information services except the richer WWW): the client, the server, the database, and the protocol. Client programs, e.g. the X Windows client xwaisq, construct queries and send them using the protocol to the appropriate server. The server responds and includes a "relevance" measure for the results of the search match to the query.

The actual operation of the protocol is quite complex, as it permits exchanges to be broken into separate parts. WAIS permits retrieval of bibliographic, as well as content (including images), data.

A search request consists of seed words, or keys if you like, typed by a user into the client, together with a list of documents (identified by a unique global

ID). The response is quite complex and includes a list of records, including the following fields:

- **Headline**   basically a title/description
- **Rank**   relative relevance of this document
- **Formats**   list of formats available (text/PostScript etc.)
- **Document ID**
- **Length**

Gopher

Gopher is a service that runs listening for TCP connections on port 70. It responds to trivial string requests from clients, with answers preceded by a single character identifying the type (as shown below), a name and a selector:

```
0    Item is a file
1    Item is a directory
2    Item is a CSO (qi) phone-book server
3    Error
4    Item is a BinHexed Macintosh file.
5    Item is DOS binary archive of some sort.
     Client must read until the TCP connection closes. Beware.
6    Item is a UNIX uuencoded file.
7    Item is an Index-Search server.
8    Item points to a text-based telnet session.
9    Item is a binary file.
     Client must read until the TCP connection closes. Beware.
+    Item is a redundant server.
T    Item points to a text-based tn3270 session.
g    Item is a GIF format graphics file.
I    Item is some kind of image file. Client decides how to display.
```

The client then chooses what to do, and how to display any actual data returned. Gopher++ is a backwards-compatible simple extension to Gopher to return more complex types of responses, including item size information, the administrator, an abstract, etc., together with the item itself. It must be said that Gopher and Gopher++ are remarkably simple and yet very powerful ways of building simple information services.

World Wide Web (WWW)

The World Wide Web makes all these previous services look like stone tablets and smoke signals. In fact, the Web is better than that. It can read stone tablets and send smoke signals too.

The World Wide Web service is made up of several components. Client programs (e.g. Mosaic, Lynx, etc.) access servers (e.g. HTTP daemons) using the protocol HTTP (HyperText Transfer Protocol). Servers hold data, written in a language called HTML. HTML is the HyperText Markup language. As indicated by its name, it is a language (in other words it consists of keywords and grammar for using them) for marking up text that is "hyper". Hyper comes from the Greek prefix meaning above or over and generally means that some additional functionality is present compared with simple text. In this case, that additional functionality is in two forms: graphics or other media and links or references to other pieces of (hyper)-text. These links are another component of the WWW, called uniform resource locators.

The pages in the World Wide Web are held in HTML format, and delivered from WWW servers to clients in this form, albeit wrapped in MIME (multipurpose Internet mail extensions) and conveyed by HTTP.

The way this all fits together is the subject of the rest of this book.

A note on stateless servers

Almost all the information servers discussed above are described as *stateless*. State is what networking people call *memory*. One of the important design principles in the Internet has always been to minimize the number of places that need to keep track of who is doing what.

In the case of stateless information servers this means that they do not keep track of which clients are accessing them. In other words, the server and protocol are constructed in such a way that, between one access and the next, they do not care who, why, how, when or where the next access will come from.

This is *essential* to the reliability of the server and to making such systems work in very large scale networks such as the Internet with potentially huge numbers of clients; if the server did depend on a client, then any client or network failure would leave the server in the lurch, possibly not able to continue, or else serving other clients with reduced resources.

In spite of this, the idea of being stateless does not necessarily mean that the servers do not keep information about clients, for example:

- **Logging how many clients and from where they access**   This can be useful even for sites that do not recoup funds for serving information, in order that they can point at the effectiveness of their information service.

- **Keeping track of most frequently accessed material** This can be useful to age and remove unaccessed information. It can also be used to decide whether to put frequently accessed information onto faster servers, or even move the information to servers nearest the most frequent clients (called *load balancing*).

- **Using access control lists to limit who can retrieve which information** Some servers allow the configuration of lists of Internet addresses, or even client users who are (or are not) permitted access to all or particular information.

- **Using authentication stages before permitting access, and also to allow billing** While we would not yet recommend using the Internet to actually carry out billing, you can certainly employ secure authentication techniques that would identify a user beyond doubt. This identification can then be used with each access log, to calculate a bill that can then be sent *out-of-band*, e.g. by post.

- **Sharing out information on heavily loaded servers or networks, differentially, depending where clients are** Some sites offer a wealth of information, but have less good long-haul Internet access. They will then distribute data more frequently in favour of local, site or national clients, before non-local or international ones.

Another use of the term *stateless* is to describe whether or not the server keeps note of the actual data from each access by a client (irrespective of whether it notes who the client was). This is called *server caching*. (Cache is usually, but not always, pronounced the same way as cash. It is nothing to do with money, or even ATM, whether ATM stands for automatic teller machine, or asynchronous transfer mode, or even another terrible mistake.)

Server caching is a way of improving the response time of a server. Usually, servers keep data on disk. If they keep a copy in memory of all the most frequently or most recently accessed data, they may be able to respond to new (or repeating) clients more quickly. Such caching is usually configurable and depends largely on measuring a whole lot of system parameters:

- **Disk speed and capacity versus memory speed and capacity** Obviously, if there is not much memory in a system, then a cache, say, of one item would have little effect.

- **Network speed versus disk speed** A memory cache is pointless if the network is always slower than the worst disk search.

- **Client access patterns** Clients may repeatedly access the same information. Different clients may tend to access the same information. Even if clients access different information over time, it may be that at one time, most people tend to access the same information (this is especially true of news servers or share information servers for example).

Caching is also employed in client programs. In other words, a client program may well not only hand each piece of information to the user – it may also squirrel away a copy of recently accessed items to avoid having to bother the server again for subsequent repeat requests for the same items.

In both server and client caching, the system should make sure that the actual master copy has not changed since the cache copy was taken. This can be quite complex.

Chapter 3
The World Wide Web

So, what is the World Wide Web?

From the user point of view, the World Wide Web is information, a great tangled web of information. Users do not care at all (well, almost not at all) about where the information is stored, about how it is stored, or about how it gets to their screens – they just say "Oh, that looks interesting", click the mouse and, after a short time (or a long time if the link is slow and the file is large), the information arrives.

We could talk all day about what the Web is like to surf, but would never give the right impression. Instead, here's a short example:

> A researcher is coming to London for a conference and she needs information on hotels to stay in. Starting with the Internet Starting Points, which is available directly from the "Navigate" menu on the screen, she might follow the a sequence like this:
>
> Selecting Internet Starting Points fetches a list of possible sources of information. See the top left corner of Figure 3.1
>
> She sees that there's a highlighted phrase that says Web Servers Directory, and she thinks "aha – maybe there's a WWW server in London". She clicks on Web Servers Directory, and after a short delay the page arrives . . .
>
> . . . On the Web Servers Directory, she searches down the list of countries until she finds the entry for the UK. One entry listed is Country Info, and she wonders what info is provided. She clicks on it and . . .
>
> . . . Country Info turns out to be an active map of the UK. She clicks on London . . .
>
> . . . and gets a guide to London, including an entry labelled Hotels in central London. She clicks on this and finds the information she was looking for.

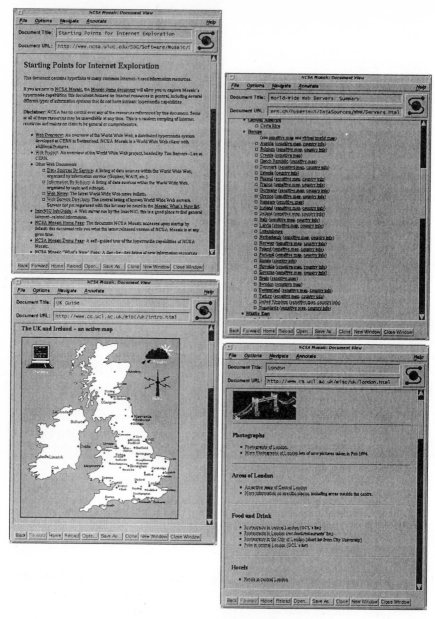

Figure 3.1 An example of browsing the World Wide Web.

She did not need to know very much information, other than where to start, and on most browsers there are a few suggested starting points built in. There are hundreds of other paths she could have followed to get to the same eventual destination.

However, this book is not about finding things in the Web, but about what happens behind the scenes in order that our researcher can find her hotel. Without high quality information in the Web, it is of no interest, but without the technology that comprises the Web, the information is unavailable. Browsing the Web is sometimes known as surfing, but what actually happens beneath the surf?

Beneath the surf

Mosaic has a few well known places to look for data built in. One of these is specified by the URL:

```
http://www.ncsa.uiuc.edu/SDG/Software/Mosaic/StartingPoints/NetworkStartingPoints
```

A URL is a uniform resource locator. This specifies what a piece of information is called

```
/SDG/Software/Mosaic/StartingPoints/NetworkStartingPoints.html,
```

where to find it (in this case the machine called www.ncsa.uiuc.edu), and which protocol to use to get the information (in this case http, or *HyperText Transfer Protocol*).

When our researcher selects Internet Starting Points, her Mosaic makes a TCP (see Chapters 1 and 2) connection to the World Wide Web server running on www.ncsa.uiuc.edu.[1] It then uses this connection to send a request for the data called NetworkStartingPoints.html. The WWW server at NCSA uses the connection to send back the requested data, and then closes down the connection.

Next, Mosaic reads various embedded commands in the data that was retrieved and creates a nicely laid out page of text, which it presents to our researcher.

Some parts of the text she sees are highlighted (on Mosaic for example, they are underlined and coloured blue). One entry she sees is:

<u>Web Servers Directory</u>: The central listing of known World Wide Web servers.

She simply clicks on the highlighted text and the associated page of informa-

---

1. www.ncsa.uiuc.edu is the Domain Name System (DNS) name of a computer called www at the ncsa (National Center for Supercomputing Applications) group of uiuc (the University of Illinois at Urbana-Champagne), which is denoted an educational institution. See Chapter 1 for more details of DNS.

tion is fetched "as if by magic". Of course, what actually happened was that the text she saw on screen was not the whole story. The page of data that was retrieved from NCSA was actually in a language called HTML or *Hyper Text Markup Language*. Before her copy of Mosaic laid out the text nicely, it actually looked something like:

```
<A HREF="http://info.cern.ch/hypertext/DataSources/WWW/Servers.html">
  Web Servers Directory
</A>: The central listing of known World Wide Web servers.
```

Thus the highlighted text she clicked on was associated with the URL:

```
http://info.cern.ch/hypertext/DataSources/WWW/Servers.html
```

and clicking on this text causes her Mosaic to make a connection to `info.cern.ch` to request the page called

```
/hypertext/DataSources/WWW/Servers.html
```

Our researcher may be sitting in Melbourne, Australia. The NCSA server is in Illinois, USA, and the CERN server is near Geneva in Switzerland, but none of this concerns our researcher – she just clicks on the highlighted items, and the hyper-links (ways of linking pieces of information together, so that when a user follows a link, she is taken from one piece of information to another related piece of information) behind them take her from server to server around the world. Unless she pays close attention to the URLs being requested, she will not know or care where the data is actually stored (except that some places have slower links than others).

On the list of places she retrieved from the CERN server, she sees the entry:

United Kingdom (**sensitive map**, **country info**)

The HTML behind (we tend to think of what we see on screen as being a front; the hard work goes on behind the scenes) this entry is actually:

```
United Kingdom
(<A HREF="http://scitsc.wlv.ac.uk/ukinfo/uk.map.html"> sensitive
  map</A>,
<A HREF="http://www.cs.ucl.ac.uk/misc/uk/intro.html"> country
  info</A>)
```

She clicks on country info, thus requesting the HTML text with the URL:

```
http://www.cs.ucl.ac.uk/misc/uk/intro.html
```

As before, her Mosaic sets up a connection, this time to `www.cs.ucl.ac.uk`, and retrieves the page called /misc/uk/intro.html. However, this time the HTML her Mosaic gets back contains the command:

```
<img src=uk_map_lbl.gif ISMAP>
```

If we ignore the ISMAP bit for a second, this says that the page should contain a GIF image at this point, and that the image is called uk_map_lbl.gif. (GIF stands for graphics interchange format, and is one form a still image can take. GIF images are relatively compact because the data is compressed, so they are quite a good format to use in the Web.) The full URL of the image is:

```
http://www.cs.ucl.ac.uk/misc/uk/uk_map_lbl.gif
```

which Mosaic can figure out from the URL of the page the image is to be contained in. Mosaic now sets up another connection to www.cs.ucl.ac.uk to request the image called /misc/uk/uk_map_lbl.gif and, when it has retrieved the image, it displays it in the correct place in the text.

Now, if it were not for the ISMAP part of this HTML, that is all that would happen – the image would be displayed and our researcher could look at it. However, in this case, the image is a map of the UK and we put some intelligence behind the map. The ISMAP part of the HTML tells our researcher's Mosaic that this image is special and it will allow her to click on the map to get more information.

In fact, the full piece of HTML we used in this particular case was:

```
<a href=/cgi-bin/imagemap/uk_map>
<img src=uk_map_lbl.gif ISMAP>
</a>
```

So, when our researcher sees London marked on the map, and she clicks on it, her Mosaic does something a little different. It sets up a connection to www.cs.ucl.ac.uk (that is where the map came from), and sends a request for the URL:

```
http://www.cs.ucl.ac.uk/cgi-bin/imagemap/uk_map?404,451
```

Here 404,451 are the co-ordinates of the point she clicked within the map. The ISMAP command associated with the image tells Mosaic to work out where the user clicked, and send that information too.[2]

At the server on www.cs.ucl.ac.uk there are a number of data files for maps. This special URL asks the server to look in its mapdata for uk_map, and find what the point 404,451 corresponds to (how this is done is described in Chapter 5).

---

2. Note that URLs used in links can be either absolute – that is they specify the protocol, the machine, the directory and the filename – or they can be relative and the unspecified parts are assumed to be the same as they are for the page containing the link.

The WWW server running on `www.cs.ucl.ac.uk` responds with the URL of the page corresponding to London on this map – in this case the URL is:

`http://www.cs.ucl.ac.uk/misc/uk/london.html`

which happens to be on the same server as the map, though it need not have been. Our researcher's Mosaic then sets up another connection to

`www.cs.ucl.ac.uk`

and requests the page `/misc/uk/london.html`. When this page is received, Mosaic parses the HTML text it gets back, and discovers the following line in the retrieved text:

`<img src=/uk/london/tower_bridge.gif>`

and so it then also requests

`http://www.cs.ucl.ac.uk/uk/london/tower_bridge.gif`

which is just a little picture of Tower Bridge in London, which does not have any special significance other than decorating the London page.

Uniform Resource Locators (URLs)

The above example presents quite a number of URLs, for instance the URL:

`http://www.cs.ucl.ac.uk/misc/uk/intro.html`

This says that the data called `/misc/uk/intro.html` can be retrieved from the server running on a computer called `www.cs.ucl.ac.uk` using HTTP, the HyperText Transfer Protocol. This could equally well say:

`http://www.cs.ucl.ac.uk:80/misc/uk/intro.html`

The number 80 here is the TCP port on the machine `www.cs.ucl.ac.uk` that the WWW server is listening on. TCP ports are a way for several different kinds of server to listen on the same machine without getting confused about which server the connection is made to (think about lots of letter boxes in an apartment block). Port 80 is the default port for the HyperText Transfer Protocol, so if you do not say which port to connect to, Mosaic and the other WWW browsers will assume that you mean port 80. Chapter 5 gives more details about server ports and why you might sometimes run a server on a different port.

URLs do not just have to specify that you use HTTP. For instance the URL:

`ftp://cs.ucl.ac.uk/mice/index`

says that to get this information, contact the FTP server running on

`cs.ucl.ac.uk.`

Most WWW browsers know how to talk to FTP servers too, so they can set up an FTP connection, and request /mice/index using the much older File Transfer Protocol.

One of the biggest plus points for Mosaic and other WWW browsers is that they are *multiprotocol clients* – that is they know about quite a number of different protocols and so they can contact a number of different types of servers for information. If the information is out there on the Internet, no matter what type of server it is on, there is almost certainly a way for a WWW browser to get it. The URL tells the browser what type of server the data resides on, and thus how to go about getting it.

Protocols that WWW browsers know about include:

- HTTP   HyperText Transfer Protocol;
- FTP   File Transfer Protocol;
- **Gopher** the menu based information system predating WWW;
- WAIS   Wide Area Information System – an information system allowing complex searching of databases
- **Telnet** the protocol that allows you to log into remote systems.
- **Archie** the indexing system that allows you to find out what information is stored where on FTP servers.

This book is primarily about the World Wide Web – to cover all of these protocols in detail would take a book several thousand pages thick, so when talking about protocols, we shall concentrate only on the native protocol spoken by WWW servers – HTTP. For more information on these other protocols and services, see Chapter 2.

An introduction to HTML

HTML is HyperText Markup Language. As indicated by its name, it is a language (in other words it consists of keywords and a grammar for using them) for marking up text that is hyper. HTML is an extension to the fairly commonly used Standard Generalized Markup Language, SGML, an ISO standard, for what that is worth.

The pages in the World Wide Web are held in HTML format, and delivered from WWW servers to clients in this form, albeit wrapped in MIME and conveyed by HTTP, of which more below.

Marking up is an ancient skill developed in the Dark Ages of publishing by guilds of printers, keen to present the written word in a pleasant and effective way on the printed page. Typically, in recent years, the skill has diminished with the advent of WYSIWYG (what you see is what you get, pronounced *whizzywig*) word-processing packages and desktop publishing systems. This need not daunt you, since you do not *have* to author or prepare material for the World Wide Web in HTML directly, unless you really want to. Typically, authors will write material using whatever word processor they are used to, and then use a filter to translate the output into HTML. We will discuss some of the various filters that are available in later chapters.

Getting started

A simple example of HTML is:

```
<HTML>
<HEAD>
<TITLE>This is the Title</TITLE>
</HEAD>
<BODY>
<H1>This is the Page Heading</H1>
This is the first paragraph.
<P>
This is another paragraph.
with a sentence
that is split over several lines in HTML.
</BODY>
</HTML>
```

When this is displayed by Mosaic, it will look like Figure 3.2.

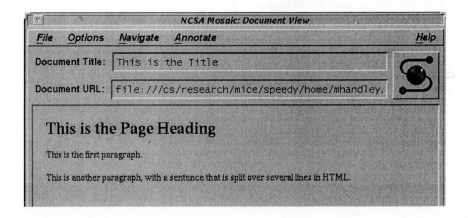

Figure 3.2 HTML display with Mosaic.

As you can probably guess, commands are enclosed in angle-brackets< >, so that the HTML command <TITLE> means that the following text is the title.

Commands beginning </ are the end of the equivalent command. For example, to say that the text "This is the Page Heading" should be a level one heading (the largest type of heading), the complete sequence is:

```
<H1>This is the Page Heading</H1>
```

A break between paragraphs is denoted <P>. There is no need for a </P> afterwards because the end of a paragraph is obvious from the start the next paragraph, list, heading or whatever.

Strictly speaking a page should start <HTML> and should end </HTML>, but the HTML specification also says that clients should perform correctly without them, and so many people omit them. Similarly the header of a document (the part containing the title) should begin with <HEAD> and end with </HEAD> and the body of a document should begin with <BODY> and end with </BODY>, but in practice this is not essential. The HEAD and BODY commands are newer additions to HTML, which allow some of the fancier features to be used, but if you are not using these features, you can safely omit both.

Documents written in HTML are not WYSIWYG – Mosaic and other WWW clients will rearrange the layout of your text so that it fits properly on whatever size display you try and display it on. So if you really want to break a line at a specific place, you should use <P>, rather than a carriage return, as Mosaic will remove the carriage return and replace it with a space and then break your line of text at a point that is convenient for the current page width. Hence the text:

```
<P>
This is another paragraph,
with a sentence
that is split over several lines.
```

will get formatted as:

This is another paragraph, with a sentence that is split over several lines.

Headings and typefaces

We have already seen one type of heading, a top-level heading denoted by the <H1> . . . </H1> pair. As you would expect, HTML supports many different levels of headers, with H1 being the largest, getting progressively smaller with H2, H3 and so on down to H6. Exactly which font and size a particular heading will be displayed with depends on which browser you use to view the text – some text based browsers will not do anything, but more fancy graphical browsers such as Mosaic will choose a sensible set of fonts; Mosaic actually lets you configure which font you want to see for each heading from your Xresources, but this is independent of the actual markup specification – see Chapter 4. HTML also lets you specify that a piece of text should be in a bold typeface using the <B> . . . </B> combination, or in an italic typeface using the <I> . . . </I> combination.

Thus the HTML:

```
<I>The</I> <B>Guardian</B> newspaper titles look like this
```

results in:

The **Guardian** newspaper titles look like this

Lists of things

Lists of things are fairly useful in ordinary text, but in HTML, where you will often have lists of links to other places, they are even more useful. However WWW servers just consisting of lists are pretty boring too, and with some imagination, you will find more interesting ways to present many things.

The simplest list is the bullet or unordered list, which is denoted by <UL>, and the list items in it are denoted using <LI>. An example is:

```
Oxymorons:
<UL>
<LI>Military Intelligence
<LI>Plastic Glasses
<LI>Moral Majority
</UL>
```

This would be displayed as:

```
Oxymorons:
•    Military Intelligence
•    Plastic glasses
•    Moral majority
```

Another form of list is the numbered or ordered list denoted by <OL>. Ordered lists have the same syntax as unordered lists except that OL replaces UL in the list delimiters:

```
Oxymorons:
<OL>
<LI>Business ethics
<LI>Chilli
</OL>
```

This gets displayed as:

Oxymorons:
1. Business ethics
2. Chilli

A more complex type of list is the definition list, denoted by <DL>. Definition terms are denoted using <DT> and actual definition data is denoted using <DD>, so a typical list may be:

```
Population Statistics:
<DL>
<DT>Ireland
<DD>population 3 million
<DT>Scotland
<DD>population 5 million
<DT>England
<PP>population too many
</DL>
```

which would be presented as:

Population Statistics:
    Ireland
        population 3 million
    Scotland
        population 5 million
    England
        population too many

If you wish to have several paragraphs of definition data associated with one definition term, simply use several <DD> entries.

Note that although the <DL> list must be finished with a </DL>, each <DT> or <DD> list item is simply ended by the next definition.

Making it all look pretty

Horizontal rules

HTML provides the <HR> command to create a horizontal line across the page – judicious use of <HR> to split a page into sections can aid readability.

Pictures

However, when it comes to attractive layout, a picture is worth a thousand words, which is fine, except for the fact that pictures generally also require a thousand times as many bytes to be transferred.

A picture can be included using an HTML command such as:

```
<img src=a_thousand_words.gif>
```

In this case, this tells Mosaic that there is a picture called

```
a_thousand_words.gif
```

on the remote server in the same directory (or folder) as this page of HTML was found in. A more complex example is:

```
<img src=http://www.cs.ucl.ac.uk/uk/london/tower_bridge.gif>
```

In this case, the image is specified with a complete URL, which tells Mosaic exactly where to go to fetch the picture. Note that the data for the picture does not need to reside on the same server as the document in which it is embedded.

Also note that we have omitted the quotes from around this URL – although it is not a bad idea to add them for the sake of clarity, or for URLs containing odd characters such as spaces, they are not strictly necessary in most circumstances.

In order for an image to be displayed in a page of a document, it must be in one of a small number of formats. However, not all formats are displayable on all browsers.

- **gif – a compressed eight-bit image format** Viewable on most browsers that support images.

- **xbm – XBitmap – two-colour uncompressed format** Viewable on most browsers that support images. The background and foreground colours on the image are typically displayed in the background and foreground colours of your browser.

- **xpm – XPixmap- multicolour X format** Not viewable on all browsers; some versions of MacMosaic cannot view this for example. The background colour is displayed in the background colour of your browser, which enables the image to merge nicely into your document.

Although many other image formats are viewable using an external viewer program, they are not necessarily viewable as embedded images on your browser. More details on MIME content types, how they are served and how the client interprets them are given in Chapters 4 and 5.

Linking it all together

We gave an example above of an image that can be stored on a different server from the text page that it is to be embedded in – this is an example of a hyperlink. Hyperlinks are what turn the Web from a not terribly good text formatting system to the tangled web of information that make the World Wide Web interesting. They are both the mechanism by which you find things and the way of tying together multiple media or data from multiple sources. The example we gave above was for an embedded image, and will be downloaded automatically, although most browsers let you delay image loading if you are working over a slow network. However, in most cases you only want the hyper link to be followed when the user clicks on it. An example is:

```
Pictures of
<A HREF=http://www.cs.ucl.ac.uk/staff/mhandley.html>Mark</A>
and
<A HREF=http://www.cs.ucl.ac.uk/staff/jon>Jon</A> are available for
those with a strong stomach.
```

This will be displayed as:

Pictures of **Mark** and **Jon** are available for those with a strong stomach.

If you now click on **Mark**, or on **Jon** you will be presented with a glorious full colour picture of one of the authors. (Fortunately this book is not yet equipped with a mouse or a radio-modem, so this is unlikely to work.)

The <A> . . . </A> in the text above denotes an anchor – in other words some additional information that has been associated with the text. In this case the anchor has a hypertext reference denoted by the keyword HREF and the URL corresponding to that reference. Other information can also be associated with an anchor – see later.

Hotlists

Users can construct indexes by creating lists of URLs. Most client programs allow people to do this easily. Many users then advertise these hotlists by adding them to their own pages in their own Web servers. Some sites keep hotlists or bookmarks organized by subject or by research interest. Some sites even let users submit new entries for their indexes. This allows navigation (although it does not really help searching) in the Web. Each hotlist or list of bookmarks represents another tour or view of the places of interest to the author of that hotlist. As more and more sites and users construct such lists, the density or value of referenced information increases.

More pretty pictures

Unfortunately, "a picture is worth a thousand words" is an understatement, and a picture is often more like the equivalent of 50,000 words, or 250 kbytes. Thus embedding large pictures in pages of text is usually not a good idea. More typical is to include a small copy of the image in the document, with a hyper link to the larger version of the image. An example would be:

```
<A HREF=big_ben.gif><IMG SRC=little_ben.gif></A>
```

In this case, it is an image `little_ben.gif` that has been given an anchor with a hyperlink to `big_ben.gif`. Mosaic will display the small image embedded in the page of text, and will only retrieve and externally display the large image `big_ben.gif` if the user should click on the small image.

Images such as the one described are called external images to distinguish them from embedded or in-line images. Most WWW browsers use a separate viewer program to display external images. On Unix systems, the most common external viewer program is *XV*. On Apple Macintoshes the external viewer is called *JPEG View*. On Windows PC's it is called *LVIEW*. Generally external viewer programs do not come bundled with the WWW browser and you will have to obtain one separately. Usually, external viewers can display a larger range of images than the WWW browser itself can, though this is changing as WWW browsers become more sophisticated. More advanced clients such as netscape do not need an external viewer at all.

Links within a page

The hyperlinks we have shown so far all take you to the top of the page at the end of the link. However, it is useful to be able to jump to specific places within a page too. For instance, where a page is quite long, it is useful to be able to have a summary of the page at the top, with hyperlinks directly to the summarized sections. This can be done by associating names with anchors as follows.

If this chapter was called `example.html` and our publisher allowed us to make it available online, we might put a list of contents at the top:

```
<UL>
    . . .
<LI> <A HREF=example.html#links>Go to Section 1</A>
<LI> <A HREF=example.html#more_pics>More Pretty Pictures</A>
<LI> <A HREF=example.html#page_links>Links Within a Page</A>
    . . .
</UL>
    . . .
<A NAME="page_links"><H2>Links Within a Page</H2></A>
The hyper links we've shown so far . . . ..
```

Now if you click in the *Links Within a Page* entry in the contents list, your browser will jump to the document with the partial URL

```
example.html# page_links.
```

As we are already viewing the document called `example.html`, it does not bother to fetch the page again, but merely jumps directly to the anchor named `page_links`.

Preformatted text

Often you will come across some preformatted plain text that you wish to put on a WWW server. You could of course go through the text and insert all the necessary HTML formatting commands, but often all you want to do is stop a WWW browser reformatting it for you. HTML provides the command pair `<PRE>` . . . `</PRE>` to delimit text that you do not want to be reformatted.

```
this text will
be reformatted
by the browser
<PRE>
and this text
will not be
reformatted
</PRE>
```

45

would look like:

this text will be reformatted by the browser
and this text
will not be
reformatted

Note that the preformatted text will be displayed in a fixed width type-writer-style font. (Typewriter-style fonts are fixed width – i.e. all the characters are the same width. Book fonts and the default fonts used by WWW clients such as Mosaic are variable-width fonts, so letters like "l" are narrower than letters like "m". Generally variable-width fonts are more pleasant to read than fixed width fonts.) You should avoid over use of <PRE>, as it does not allow WWW browsers any leeway in doing anything clever about line wrapping, and because typewriter-style fonts are generally quite ugly.

A note on links

In the examples above, we have shown two forms of links – an absolute URL such as is used in this image link:

    <img src=http://www.cs.ucl.ac.uk/uk/london/tower_bridge.gif>

and relative links such as:

    <img src=tower_bridge.gif>

If this relative link is in a page of HTML with the URL

    http://www.cs.ucl.ac.uk/uk/london/index.html

then the client assumes that the protocol (http), the remote computer (www.cs.ucl.ac.uk) and the directory (/uk/london) are all the same as those in the page containing the link, and so it actually requests the data with the absolute URL

    http://www.cs.ucl.ac.uk/uk/london/tower_bridge.gif

Another possibility is to specify relative URLs with the full directory and filename – the client knows that you mean this because the directory name begins with a slash (/). For example, the relative link above could have also been written:

    <img src=/uk/london/tower_bridge.gif>

You can even use relative directory names using Unix-style relative path-names. For example, an HTML page with the URL

```
http://www.cs.ucl.ac.uk/uk/intro.html
```

could use the following link the same picture of Tower Bridge:

```
<img src=london/tower_bridge.gif>
```

and an HTML page with the URL:

```
http://www.cs.ucl.ac.uk/uk/london/east_end/docks.html
```

could use a link such as:

```
<img src=../tower_bridge.html>
```

Note that the ../ here refers to the parent directory of the current directory in the directory tree. The parent directory of a directory is the directory above it in the file system tree. On a Macintosh, you may think of the parent folder of a particular folder as being the folder that contains it.

Special characters

As HTML uses a number of characters to denote its own commands, you will have problems if you try to actually put these characters in your HTML and expect them to display properly. To get around this problem, HTML provides some special character entities. These are always prefixed by an ampersand (&) and followed by a semicolon (;) as shown:

<   The "less than" sign <
>   The "greater than" sign >
& The ampersand sign & itself
" The double quote sign "
  A non-breaking space

Also, if the text you are writing is not in the English language, you will probably need to use a number of accented characters. HTML allows you to do this in the same way. The full list allowed by HTML is given as part of the HTML grammar in Appendix A.

Where are we now?

Now that we have a good understanding of the use of the Web and the form of the information in it (HTML), we need to look at how clients and servers work and talk to each other. That is the subject of the next two chapters.

Chapter 4
Client programs

In this chapter, we take a user's look at Mosaic (for DOS and Unix), and the line/screen mode client Lynx. There are numerous other clients, emerging even as we write. A shortlist includes:

- perl WWW   a terminal based fast simple browser;
- Emacs W3-mode   for Gnus;
- Cello   for PCs;
- WinWeb   for PC/DOS systems;
- Albert   for VM systems;
- MacWeb and MacMosaic   for Apple Macintosh systems;
- NetScape   for Unix, Windows and Macintoshes;
- Wordia, the Microsoft Internet Assistant   for Windows.

What does a WWW browser program actually do?

A WWW client or browser (we use the terms client and browser interchangeably) connects to a WWW server and asks for a document. It knows which server to connect to and which document to ask for from the information given in a URL (see Chapters 3 and 5). When the server replies with the contents of the document, the client must display it to the user.

A document can contain plain text to be displayed, it can contain HTML text that needs special formatting or it can contain multimedia data such as a picture or an audio clip to be displayed or played. The client must decide what type of data the document contains and hence what to do with it. The information about what type of data the document contains is conveyed in a few additional lines of information that the WWW server adds to the top of the document. In particular, the line that says what type of data is in the document is called the content type (see the section below on *Configuring MIME types for launching viewers* and the section on MIME in Chapter 5 for more details).

Some content types, such as plain text or HTML text, will be dealt with by the client itself. Plain text is easy to display. HTML takes a little more intelligence, as it needs laying out neatly on the screen in appropriate fonts and the paragraphs of text need to be wrapped at appropriate places if the screen is too narrow to display them. HTML can also contain embedded images (see next section). As embedded images need not necessarily be stored on the same server as the document they are embedded in, to display an embedded image the browser may need to make another connection to a server to retrieve the image data (returned with an image content type), and then leave enough space in the text to insert the picture. Figure 4.1 shows an example.

Figure 4.1   EIT MacWeb displaying images on an Apple Macintosh.

Some links in an HTML document will also result in documents being retrieved that contain data that cannot be displayed by the browser itself. In most cases the browser will then send the document data to a separate viewer program to display the image or play the video or audio clip that the document data represents (we still speak of a viewer program even when we are "viewing" audio). See the section below on configuring MIME types for how a browser knows which viewer to start up.

Displaying embedded images

Not all client programs are able to display images embedded in a document – a browser such as Lynx (see Figure 4.5) is character based not graphical, and so cannot display images in line. However, all graphical browsers can display images embedded in pages of HTML and, when they download a page of HTML containing references to embedded images, they will automatically connect to the relevant server and download the image data.

If your network connection is fast, you will probably want embedded images downloaded and displayed automatically. However, if your network connection is slow, waiting for (and possibly paying for) images to be downloaded can be annoying. Because of this, most clients let you delay image loading until the user specifically asks for an image (Figure 4.2).

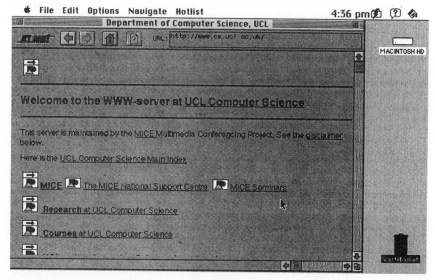

Figure 4.2   Delayed image loading with MacWeb.

Most versions of Mosaic use the symbol shown in Figure 4.3 (or one similar to) it to indicate an image whose loading has been deferred. The image will be downloaded and displayed in line if you click on it.

Figure 4.3   Delayed image loading.

If there is an in-line image whose loading has been deferred, and there was also a link from the embedded image to another document or image, then Mosaic uses the symbol shown in Figure 4.4. If you click on the bottom part of the symbol, the in-line image will be downloaded and displayed as usual. If you click on the top arrow part of the symbol, Mosaic will follow the link without bothering to download the in-line image.

Figure 4.4   Delayed image loading with a link from the image.

Text-based clients will usually indicate in some way that there would have been an embedded image in the document, but there is not much they can do to display it. Lynx will put [image] at the place in the text where there would have been an image (see Figure 4.5). However HTML also allows you to specify a text string to be displayed on non-graphical browsers and Lynx will display this text string in place of [image] if it is given.

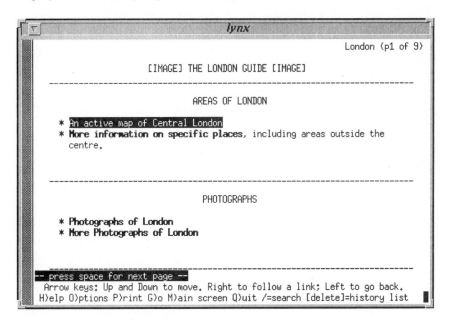

Figure 4.5   Lynx – an example of a text-based browser.

When designing pages of HTML, you should try to bear in mind the limitations of different browsers, and if the contents of an image are important for understanding a page (such as the heading on our London guide – see Figures 4.1 and 4.5), then, when possible, an alternative text string should also be given.

Running a client

To retrieve data from a WWW server, a WWW client needs to be able to communicate with it. Typically, a client is a standalone program that relies on some underlying communications package. On a Unix or Windows-NT system this is built into the basic operating system. On an MS-Windows system or an Apple Macintosh, it is not built in as standard, and you may need to install the networking software too. There are many excellent guides on how to do this, and your Internet provider may even do it for you. In the MS-Windows case you will also need to tell the browser where to find the networking software – this is described later in this chapter.

The client is a fairly complex system, which not only accesses WWW servers across the network using HTTP, but must also understand the MIME and HTML in any responses (and any HTTP error responses too). Its main task is to display as well as possible the documents you access. Typically, the client application does not comprehend all the many different media, text, graphics, audio, video, etc., since that would make it an enormous, monolithic program, possibly unable to run on any but the most powerful workstations. Instead, it is designed to launch the appropriate viewers for the appropriate media types according to a set of configuration information based on the MIME set-up for reading multimedia mail.

Different browsers and different viewing styles

Figures 4.1 and 4.5 to 4.10 show a range of WWW client programs. Although we cannot possibly list all the available browsers here, the following are some of the most popular:
 • EIT MacWeb running on an Apple Macintosh (Fig. 4.1);
 • Lynx, a text based browser running on Unix systems (Fig. 4.5);
 • NCSA Mosaic running on an Apple Macintosh (Fig. 4.6);
 • NCSA Mosaic running on an MS-Windows PC (Fig. 4.7);
 • EIT WinWeb running on an MS-Windows PC (Fig. 4.8);
 • The original NCSA Mosaic running on a Unix machine under the X Window system (Fig. 4.9);
 • Netscape running on a Unix machine under the X Window system (Fig. 4.10).

As you can see, these clients (at least, the graphical ones anyway) have a lot in common, and if you are used to using one of them, you will find that the others are all fairly similar. However, each has a different set of constraints and all manage to display the same page of HTML subtly differently.

At the time of writing, Netscape is the most technically advanced of these clients, though no doubt the others will catch up fast. Most clients will down-

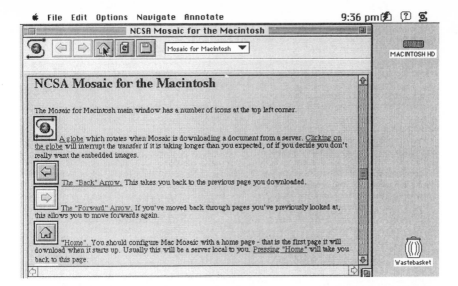

Figure 4.6   NCSA Mosaic on an Apple Macintosh.

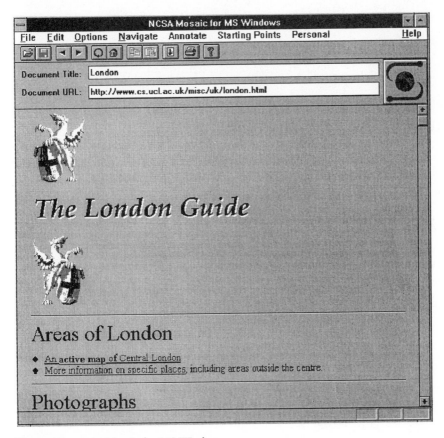

Figure 4.7   NCSA Mosaic for MS Windows.

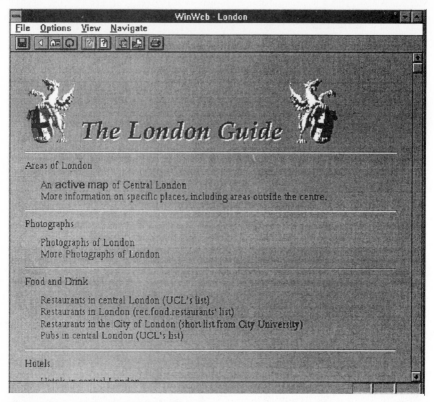

Figure 4.8 EIT WinWeb for MS Windows.

load images one after another. Some (for example Mosaic for X) will wait until all the images have been downloaded before displaying the page. Others will display the text and then as they complete each image load, they will add it to the page being displayed. Netscape is even more fancy – it can download images from different servers simultaneously and display parts of images that have been received – so you get the best possible performance, as long as you are not limited by your local network bandwidth, and you get to see the data you have retrieved as soon as possible. Netscape also displays so-called "external" images in its own main window. However, this is not always what is desired.

As HTML continues to evolve, some clients will implement new features before others. Not so long ago, active map handling and forms were new features only supported by a few clients. Now they are almost standard. There is no doubt that we will continue to see new features for some time to come, but they should be implemented in such a way that old clients do not actually break down, although they also will not do the right thing. If you are using one of the public domain clients such as NCSA Mosaic, all you need to do is retrieve the new version free of charge.

Figure 4.9   Mosaic for X (running on a Sun).

A simple user guide

As you can see, no one book can hope to provide a user guide for all the exist-ing clients, let alone guess how they will evolve. Here, we will try to extract

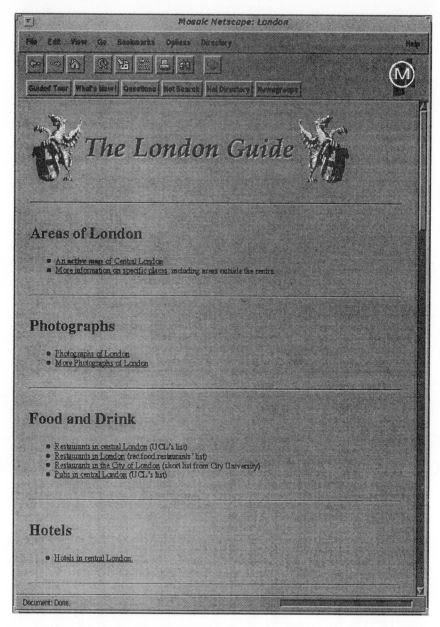

Figure 4.10   Netscape (running on a Sun).

the common functionality that applies to most of the WWW browsers mentioned in the previous section.

When you run a WWW browser, it will automatically load a "home" page (see below). This will consist of text, possibly a few images and links to other documents. Text that possesses a link to another document is usually underlined and highlighted, either in bold, or in another colour from the rest of the text. Images that possess a link to another document have a highlighted border to distinguish them from images without links. If you click the mouse on the linked image or text, the browser will retrieve the linked document. This is the basic way of browsing the Web – you simply click on text that possesses links (so called "hot" text), and travel from place to place around the Web. To start browsing the Web, this really is all you need to know.

Jumping from document to document using hotspots (links) is like learning to walk – it is simple and it lets you get anywhere. However, although walking is simple and effective, walking by itself is not everything – for instance, you need to remember where you have just been ("This road doesn't look as interesting as the one back there – how do I get back there"), you need to remember how to get to places you have been before ("I think I got there this way last week!") and when you have to go a long way, walking's not as fast as getting on a plane ("Do I have to walk to China again? I did that last week! There must be a faster way!"). To help you, WWW browsers provide a number of memory aids and short cuts. The following are a few of the basic ones (Fig. 4.11):

- **Home**   For when you really get lost, or when you decide you are not getting anywhere and want to try again, browsers provide a "Home" button that returns you directly to your home page (see below).

- **Back**   When you are browsing you will often see a link that looks interesting, and follow it. Several links later, you will realize that was not what you were looking for after all. Pressing "Back" repeatedly will retrace your steps back towards where you came from.

- **Forward**   As the name suggests, this is the reverse of "Back". Usually used when you have pressed "Back" one too many times. Smart browsers will keep a copy of the pages you have seen, and so you will not have to reload them as you move backwards and forwards.

- **Open URL**   URLs are the World Wide Web's addresses. If you know a URL, most browsers let you type it in and then take you straight there. Often people email each other URLs of interesting information to save having to mail all the actual information itself.

- **Hotlist**   This is your own private list of interesting places. When you find a place you will want to visit again, add it to your hotlist so that you will be able to find it again (this saves typing in URLs every time).

Figure 4.11   Icons in Mosaic for X (running on a Sun).

Most browsers also let you print pages out and save them to disk in a number of formats. Another feature often provided is "Reload", which is very useful if you are developing HTML and have to keep loading the same page until you get it right.

Configuring MIME types for launching viewers

When a WWW server returns a document to a WWW client, it specifies the type of the data contained in the document using a MIME content type (see below). The client will be able to handle some MIME content types itself, but it is unlikely to be able to handle all possible content types, so it will have to feed the data to another program that can.

Most clients come with a built in set of default programs to handle specific common content types, but you may also want to add a new content type, or simply tell the client to use a different program to display a particular content type. In this case, you will have to tell the client which application to run to view that particular content type.

For example, if an HTTP request returns the MIME content type

```
application/postscript
```

your client needs to know that it should launch the PostScript previewer, say GhostScript. This is done using a "mailcap" or *mail capability file*, taken from the MIME standards (see RFC 1521 and Appendix D). Note that, if you change your mailcap file, you may need to restart your client program before it will recognize the changes.

Here is an example mailcap file:

```
# any line with a `#´ at the beginning is a comment
# This causes us to use mpeg_play_x to view MPEG
video/mpeg; mpeg_play_x %s
# This is our default audio player program
audio/basic; showaudio %s
# This is useful for the
audio/x-illustrated; iaunpack %s
```

Note that such personal customization is usually in addition to the system-wide default mailcap.

A very powerful, and dangerous, feature of some clients is the ability to have the server cause the execution of arbitrary programs at the client end (this is the exact inverse of the Common Gateway Interface or CGI, which is discussed in Chapter 5). This can be done by the server returning a MIME content type application/x-csh and a mailcap file with this appropriately configured:

```
# Danger Danger Danger - extreme security loophole potential!!!
application/x-csh; csh -f %s
```

A safer option for servers providing such *active* information is to use languages such as *perl* or *Tcl* that are available in safe forms and where the interpreter can check for file access or the execution of specific commands.

Starting points, history and hotlists

When you first unwrap your new birthday present, you play with it a lot. Likewise, when you first run a WWW client like Mosaic, the tendency is to browse a lot. One of the things you will find is that there are a number of well-known starting points in the Web for exploring. However, as you visit more and more places and find them useful, you will find you want to save their locations. Typically, a client will let you file away a URL with its title in a Hotlist.

Sometimes, as a result of the web-like nature of WWW (as opposed to simple tree-like menu systems: remember the computer in Jurassic Park?), you can get lost. Most clients let you keep a history, both for the current session and globally.

Your home page

When you start up a WWW browser, it will download a document automatically. If no-one has done any configuration on your browser, it will probably download the home page for your particular WWW browser, which will no doubt contain a few links to other useful places in the Web.

Using the default home page is not something that we would recommend though. The WWW server that provides the default homepage is probably getting huge numbers of requests per minute and so will not be very fast. In addition, the links it has are probably not to places that you will want to access very often. If you have a WWW server at your site, you should probably configure your browser to use your site's home page. Even if you do not have a WWW server, you can always set up a file of HTML on the machine on which you run your browser to be your own private home page, complete with links to things you find interesting.

Most Unix browsers will use the WWW_HOME environment variable to decide where their home page is. Mac and PC browsers usually let you set the home page from the user interface as a "preference".

To set up a home page on your local disk, create the file of HTML you want to use (for example home.html on the MACINTOSH HD) complete with links to places you want to visit often, and then set your home page to:

```
file:///MACINTOSH HD/home.html
```

Personal annotations

Sometimes, you may want to make notes about some information you find in the WWW. Many clients let you annotate a Web page (some even let you use audio or even video, though most are text based). The client tool then simply keeps a note of the URL and, when you visit it again, reminds you that you have an annotation by displaying the fact (and a hot pointer in the display area), so you can retrieve it. Fear not! You are not altering someone else's data; just keeping a personal note.

Customizing your view of the Web

Most clients allow you to customize the way they display the marked-up page that you have retrieved. This is a bone of contention between some people about WWW; the fact that individuals may see the author's data in very different ways seems curious in the extreme to people from the publishing world, where standards of layout are very fixed (and high). If you want to put information in the Web in an immutable way, then using some image or PostScript or similar approach may be more appropriate.

At the very least, a system will let you change the way it displays anchors and, possibly globally, the type of font used. Most graphical clients let you delay or prevent image loading, so that they are usable over slow links, though not everyone who provides information on the Web appreciates how this affects the look of a page. Of course text-based clients such as Lynx cannot display in-line images anyway.

Common Client Interface

Some clients can be controlled by other programs through some external communications mechanism. A WWW standard for this mechanism is still under development, but Mosaic and Netscape have their own ways of doing it.

You can direct the Mosaic Unix client to visit a particular URL by sending it messages – the Unix approach is simply to place a command in a temporary file called

```
/tmp/Mosaic.pid
```

where *pid* is the process id of the Mosaic client found by running the command to get a process status listing (e.g. ps). You then use the Unix signal facility to prompt Mosaic to take notice

```
kill -USR1 1234
```

where 1234 is the process id of Mosaic. Commands span two lines and look like:

```
goto
http://www.cs.ucl.ac.uk/people/jon.html
```

To do the same thing with Netscape, you simply run another Netscape and give it a command line argument.

```
netscape -remote "openURL(http://www.cs.ucl.ac.uk/staff/jon)"
```

This makes use of the underlying X windows system to carry the message.

A portable, system-independent CCI mechanism is at the design stage at the time of writing.

Accessing other information services through client programs

You do not have to do anything special from most WWW clients to access other information servers directly. Most clients have the protocol built in. For example, Mosaic understands FTP, the Telnet protocol, Gopher, WAIS, News and local file access.

Of course, many of these will become obsolete as people design better gateways from servers, freeing up the clients to concentrate on clean efficient handling of HTTP, MIME and HTML. The rise of *proxy servers* such as CERN's HTTPD 3.0 mean that even a pure HTTP client could have access to FTP, Gopher and so forth.

Viewing HTML source documents from a client

One of the more useful tricks of the trade in WWW is to learn new and sensible ways (or even old and bad ways) of designing pages in HTML by looking at other people's source documents. If you find a well designed page, use Mosaic (or another client) to access the HTML source of the page, and (preferably) look at it side by side with the formatted page. Beware, though, that if the page has been generated by a filter (see Chapter 6) it may be weird and not terribly readable for humans.

PC/MS-DOS clients

While there are not likely to be sophisticated servers for an MS-DOS environment, there are plenty of good client programs. One of the complications of DOS is the fact that it has not been a networked operating system. While this is different for Windows-NT and will be true for newer MS Windows users, older MS Windows or MS-DOS users must provide their own networking. In fact, without Windows, the best option for an MS-DOS user is to buy dial-up Internet access and use a line-mode client like Lynx on the dial-up Internet host. However, Windows tasking and networking are rapidly becoming available, making full access from GUI clients a lot easier.

There are a number of public-domain or low-cost networking packages that run under MS Windows. Most conform to the emerging *winsock* network application programming interface (API). Winsock has the massive advantage that it is very closely compatible with the most widely used Unix networking API, the so-called BSD sockets interface. This means that a widely used client, NCSA's Mosaic, has been ported to the Windows environment on PCs.

The configuration below is a subset of a tested one that works with Mosaic 2.0. The fields are largely self-explanatory. Also, many of these can be set from the application:

```
[Main]
E-mail="jon@cs.ucl.ac.uk"
Autoload Home Page=yes
Home Page=http://www.cs.ucl.ac.uk/index.html/
Display Inline Images=yes
[Viewers]
TYPE0="audio/wav"
TYPE1="application/postscript"
TYPE2="image/gif"
TYPE3="image/jpeg"
TYPE4="video/mpeg"
TYPE8="audio/x-midi"
telnet="c:\trumpet\telw.exe"
[Suffixes]
application/postscript=.ps,.eps,.ai,.ps
text/html=
text/plain=
application/x-rtf=.rtf,.wri
audio/wav=.wave,.wav,.WAV
audio/x-midi=.mid
image/x-tiff=.tiff,.tif
image/jpeg=.jpeg,.jpe,.jpg
video/mpeg=.mpeg,.mpe,.mpg
```

Trumpet Winsock

Just to prove we tested this, the configuration file (trumpwsk.ini) from the PC running the above Mosaic configuration is:

```
[Trumpet Winsock]
ip    = 128.16.8.188
netmask = 255.255.240.0
gateway = 128.16.6.150
dns   = 128.16.5.31
time  =
domain = cs.ucl.ac.uk
vector = 00
mtu   = 1500
rwin  = 4096
mss   = 1460
slip-enabled  = 0
slip-port     = 2
slip-baudrate  = 2400
slip-handshake = 1
slip-compressed = 0
dial-option   = 0
online-check  = 0
inactivity-timeout = 5
slip-timeout  = 0
registration-name = ""
registration-password = "h[G?"Rg]"
```

These configuration parameters are *very* site specific, so please change them in accordance with your Internet provider's instructions. The first three fields and the sixth (domain=) are specific to your machine, and using the ones in this example will not work. The domain name server (dns=) indicated is also not really a good guess for this field, although it will in fact serve. The other fields are for workable performance over an Ethernet. If you are using Slip, enable the slip lines and set the port and baud rate to be appropriate to the modem you are using. If you are on a 2400 baud dial-up line, it is advisable to change the Mosaic.ini file to unset the Display In-line Images field, as this will tie up the line and make WWW performance less pleasant.

Internet Assistant

The Microsoft Internet Assistant (IA) is one of the latest additions to the suite of client programs for WWW access. IA is a very cute add-on to Word for Windows (version 6.0a or later) that permits the user to access WWW servers from within the Word application. Basically, the PC must have a TCP/IP winsock compliant stack installed, and then IA intercepts accesses to URLs and turns them into HTTP requests to the appropriate server.

IA is a bit more than just a client. It also incorporates an HTML editor, and the ability to write Word documents that include embedded URLs. Thus one can author and view the WWW from one and the same application. This gives it an immense advantage over other clients since the user does not have to learn a new interface or word-processing package. It is only a matter of time before other Microsoft applications such as Powerpoint, Excel, and even Apple applications follow suit.

LibWWW – writing your own client

The *de facto* communications-layer API is sockets or winsock. There is also a convenient communications layer for WWW access for clients, based on the approach taken at CERN. There is a clean C library called LibWWW, with which it would be relatively straightforward to implement your own client program with your own GUI. However, this is really outside the scope of this book, which is primarily aimed at information users and providers rather than programmers.

Local file access

Mosaic on Unix needs to know what file holds what kind of data. The following table shows the defaults for mappings between its understanding of a MIME type and the file extension used normally to convey this.

Default File Extensions in Mosaic

```
.mime    message/rfc822
.ps      application/postscript
.html    text/html
.c       text/plain
.cc      text/plain
.c++     text/plain
.h       text/plain
.text    text/plain
.tex     text/plain
```

```
.pl       text/plain
.txt      text/plain
.snd      audio/basic
.au       audio/basic
.aiff     audio/x-aiff
.aifc     audio/x-aiff
.tar      application/octet-stream
.uu       application/octet-stream
.saveme   application/octet-stream
.dump     application/octet-stream
.bin      application/octet-stream
.gif      image/gif
.tif      image/x-tiff
.tiff     image/x-tiff
.jpg      image/jpeg
.jpeg     image/jpeg
.mpg      video/mpeg
.mpeg     video/mpeg
.hdf      application/x-hdf
.cdf      application/x-netcdf
.nc       application/x-netcdf
.dvi      application/x-dvi
.xwd      image/x-xwd
.rgb      image/x-rgb
.rtf      application/x-rtf
.pdf      application/x-pdf
.src      application/x-wais-source
.wsrc     application/x-wais-source
```

Note: Extension mapping in Mosaic is case insensitive.

Chapter 5

Serving information to the Web

If you just want to use the Web as an information source, you do not need to know about WWW servers; you only need to run a client such as Mosaic to browse everyone else's information. However, if you want to present your own information on the Web, you will either need to run a WWW server yourself or hire space on someone else's server.

It is worth noting again that you can use WWW technology for organizing information within a single machine, as well as providing information over a private network, provided it uses the appropriate protocols.

WWW servers

A WWW Server is a piece of software running on a computer that listens on a TCP port (usually port 80) for incoming connections from clients. It expects a connecting client to speak a protocol called HTTP or *HyperText Transfer Protocol*. The connecting client is usually a browser such as Mosaic, which will request some information from the server, and the server will then return the requested information to the client, subject to the client passing any security restrictions the server may have.

HTTP is a fairly simple protocol, and if you want to see what actually happens, you can *Telnet* to a WWW server and talk to it yourself. (This can often by used to attempt to debug a misbehaving server. However, some servers do not check their input too carefully, and it may be possible to crash them by typing incorrect HTTP commands.) The simplest HTTP request is GET. An example of Telnetting to a server and issuing a GET request is:

```
telnet> open macpb1.cs.ucl.ac.uk 80
Connected to macpb1.cs.ucl.ac.uk
Escape character is '^]'.
GET /index.html HTTP/1.0

HTTP/1.0 200 OK
MIME-Version: 1.0
Server: MacHTTP
Content-type: text/html

<title>Mark's Powerbook on the Web</title>
<h1>Welcome to Mark's WWW server</h1>
This temporary server is running on an Apple Macintosh
Powerbook 180 using MacHTTP 1.3.
There's not much here right now, except for the
<a href=Default.html>HTTP documentation</a>.
```

The request I made was GET /index.html and as an additional parameter, I told the server I spoke HTTP/1.0. The server responded with the document index.html, and also with some additional information. The first line of the response says that the server is also speaking HTTP/1.0, that the status code my request returned was 200, which in human terms means OK. The next line gives information about the version of MIME (see next section). Then there is a line that says what type of server this was. And finally there is a line that says the Content-Type is text/html. This last line is actually giving the MIME content type, which is how the server tells the client what to do with the information that follows. In this case it says that what follows is actually text (as opposed to an image, video, audio or a whole host of other possibilities), and that this particular text is in HTML format. If we had asked for this information using a WWW client instead of Telnet, the client would have read the Content-type line, and known to feed the data following into its HTML interpreter.

MIME

MIME stands for Multipurpose Internet Mail Extensions and was originally designed for sending multimedia electronic mail. The two main things it does are specify in a standard way what type of media the content of a message actually is and in what form it has been encoded for transmission. When Tim Berners-Lee was originally designing what would go on to become the World Wide Web, he had exactly this same requirement – he needed a server to be able to specify to a client what a response contained and how it had been encoded. However, the email people (Nathaniel Borenstein and Ned Freed) had got there first and had already specified MIME, so there was no need to reinvent the wheel, even though for this purpose the name is a little odd.

MIME content types

MIME content types consist of a type (such as text) and a subtype (such as html).

The most common MIME types relevant to the WWW are:

- A text content type, which is used to represent textual information in a number of character sets and formatted text description languages in a standardized manner. The two most likely subtypes are:
  - text/plain   text with no special formatting requirements;
  - text/html   text with embedded HTML commands.

- An application content type, which is used to transmit application data or binary data. Two frequently used subtypes are:
  - application/binary   the data is in some unknown binary format, such as the results of a file transfer;
  - application/postscript   the data is in the PostScript language and should be feed to a PostScript interpreter.

- An image content type, for transmitting still image (picture) data. There are many possible subtypes, but the ones used most often on the Web are:
  - image/gif   an image in the GIF format;
  - image/xbm   an image in the XBitmap format;
  - image/jpeg   an image in the JPEG format.

- An audio content type, for transmitting audio or voice data.
  - audio/basic   the data consists of 8 kHz 8 bit mu-law audio samples. This is the standard way that audio is encoded digitally for the telephone system in the USA and Japan, and, because of this, many inexpensive hardware devices now exist on computers for input and output in this form. Basically, the analogue audio is sampled in 8 bit chunks 8000 times a second and each chunk assigned a "pulse" value. mu-law refers to the way the "sound" of the pulse is converted to an 8 bit value.

- A video content type, for transmitting video or moving image data, possibly with audio as part of the composite video data format:
  - video/mpeg   the data is MPEG format video;
  - video/quicktime   the data is QuickTime format video.

Suffixes, servers and MIME types

Now we know how a server tells a client what type of information is being returned, but how does the server figure out this information?

In the Unix and DOS worlds, files are usually identified using file name suffixes. In the DOS world they are limited to three characters, but on Unix systems they can be any length. Thus a file called london_zoo.gif is likely to be an image in the GIF format. Servers typically have a set of built-in suffixes that they assume denote particular content types. They also let you specify the content types of your own suffixes in case you have any local oddities, or something new that the server designer had not thought of.

On Apple Macintoshes, most users are used to being able to call files whatever they want, and the resource information associated with the file specifies which application created it and what its file type is. Although MacHTTP can use the Mac file type to specify the content type, what happens with data that did not originate on a Mac? To solve this, MacHTTP has a similar configuration file and also lets you use Unix-style suffixes to specify the MIME content type to report back to clients.

URLs and server file systems

WWW servers generally reside on machines with a file system (a proxy server need not have a file system, but most do). The server's job is to make part of that file system publicly available by responding to HTTP requests. Its job is also to prevent the private parts of that file system from becoming public.

Most file systems can be thought of as a form of tree, and the URLs used in the WWW also use this model. Thus the URL:

http://www.cs.ucl.ac.uk/misc/uk/london.html

specifies the file called london.html, which is in a directory called uk, which in turn is in a directory called misc, which resides in the top level directory of the tree (or *root*, as it is often called – as if the tree were the normal way up); root is sometimes simply called "/" ("*slash*") (see Fig. 5.1).

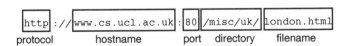

Figure 5.1   The structure of a uniform resource locator.

The slashes ("/") separating the directory names are the Unix way of specifying a file name. On DOS and Windows systems, users are more used to back slashes ("\"). Many Apple Mac users are not familiar with this concept at all, although their folders do actually perform the same task. Although users do not often see it, Apple scripts use the colon (":") where Unix uses a slash. However, when you are writing URLs, whatever system you are on, you must use slashes. If you are more used to folders than directories, simply substitute the word "folder" wherever we say "directory".

When the URL above specifies /misc/uk/london.html, this does not usually mean that the misc directory is really situated in the root directory ("/") of the entire file system. Instead it is situated in the root directory of the subtree that the WWW server makes public. Any documents situated in this subtree are accessible to the server, and directories that are not in this subtree are not accessible (see Fig. 5.2).

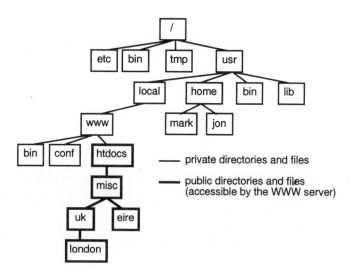

Figure 5.2 A WWW server makes a subtree of the filesystem public.

With some servers this is the whole story. However, most servers also allow you to provide some form of access control to files and subdirectories of the visible subtree. This protection can take the form of restrictions on the machines or networks from which a client can access a file or it may be password protection. Which mechanisms a server provides depend on which server you choose, and we will discuss a few of the better servers in Chapter 8.

Another issue is raised when a server is running on a machine in a large multi-user environment such as a university. For instance, each student in a university can write files to their own file store, but not anywhere else. However, we would like our students to be able to create their own WWW pages, despite not having access to the WWW server's default public tree. WWW server designers have foreseen this need and Unix servers usually make available files placed in a special directory in the user's home directory. On NCSA and CERN servers, this directory is called `public_html` by default. Thus accesses to the URL

`http://www.euphoric-state-uni.edu/~janet/research/index.html`

would map onto the file:

`/usr/home/janet/public_html/research/index.html`

in the file system shown in Figure 5.3.

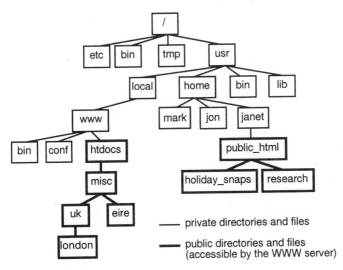

Figure 5.3   A WWW server exporting a user's `public_html` pages.

Once we start to allow the WWW server access to areas of our file system that can be modified by users whom we do not necessarily trust, a whole set of security issues is raised. For example, Unix allows symbolic links from one place in the directory tree to another in order to give the impression that files or directories are somewhere else (on a Mac symbolic links are called "Aliases"). Letting the server follow links can be useful, but it also can create problems. Just because a file is readable by other users on your own system does not necessarily mean that it should be readable by users on other sites or in other countries.

In Figure 5.4, we see that Janet has made a symbolic link from inside her `public_html` subtree to John's `new_project` directory, making it accessible to the whole world without John's knowledge. Most servers allow different security options to be specified on a per subtree basis, and in this case, if following symbolic links had been switched off for `public_html` directories, the problem would have been avoided. MacHTTP simply prohibits the following of links, which is another way to solve the problem.

71

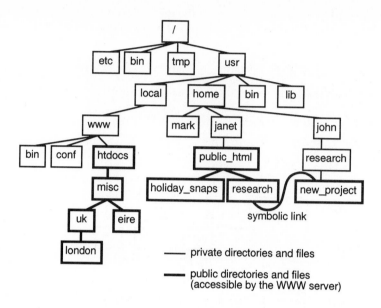

Figure 5.4   Problems with a WWW server following symbolic links.

Proxy servers

If you have used a WWW client such as Mosaic, you have probably already used a proxy *client*. Mosaic and other clients built upon LibWWW can contact servers for protocols such as FTP and Gopher, and then convert the output of such servers into HTML for formatting and display on your screen (see Fig. 5.5). Proxy servers take this one step further; instead of your client contacting remote servers directly, your client makes an HTTP request to a proxy server. The proxy server then contacts the relevant FTP or Gopher server, and converts the results to HTML, before transferring them back to your client (see Fig. 5.6).

A proxy server can also make connections to remote HTTP servers. At first glance, this does not appear to benefit you, as the proxy then performs no conversion, but it provides a way to provide network services to machines on a secure subnet without those machines having to have direct access to the outside world. Thus, secure sites can run a proxy server on their firewall ma-

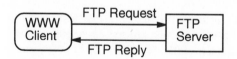

Figure 5.5   A WWW proxy client contacting an FTP server.

chine, or socksify only their proxy server without needing to modify the WWW client programs for all their different architectures (see Fig. 5.7). "Socksify" is the term used for taking a communications program written using the socket or winsock API, and making it more secure using a public domain package called "socks". This package allows a server to be reached indirectly, so that it can operate behind a firewall. A firewall is a router (or system of routers) that performs a number of extra checks to a site, making it potentially more secure.

Even if you do not need this level of security, CERN's HTTPD can also provide caching facilities for clients using the server as a proxy. Caching facilities

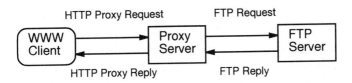

Figure 5.6 An FTP proxy server answering an HTTP request.

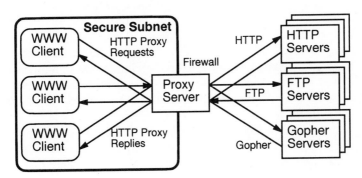

Figure 5.7 A proxy server on a firewall.

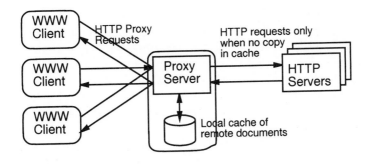

Figure 5.8 A caching proxy server.

73

in the World Wide Web are currently in their infancy, as many servers do not return expiry date information with documents, so deciding how long data should be cached before going back to look at the original is not a clear cut issue. However, CERN's server uses whatever information is available to it to make a decision about cache timeouts and, although it does not always do the right thing, it does substantially improve performance for frequently accessed pages and most of the time it gets it right (see Fig. 5.8).

Server scripts

If the World Wide Web merely permitted the retrieval of hypertext files, it might have still been popular, but it is the ability to define new programs to be run in the server when a request is made that really makes the Web flexible and fun. An example is an active map, where a user clicks on a map and the place they clicked is sent to the server along with their request. The server then runs a program or script that figures out where those co-ordinates apply to and, depending on where the user clicked, it sends back the relevant next page of information (see Chapter 3 for an example, or the next section for details of how to write active maps on various servers).

Active maps are just one example; what you can do with server scripts is really only limited by your imagination. An interesting example is Cambridge University's coffee machine – there is a video camera pointed at the coffee pot and a server script captures a picture of it using a video frame grabber, and sends the image to you so that you can see whether there is any coffee ready.

A standard called Common Gateway Interface (CGI), has emerged for the writing of server scripts and is supported by most servers. This means that scripts written for one server should easily be ported to another server.

Common Gateway Interface (CGI)

CGI, the Common Gateway Interface, is a standardized way of writing scripts that the server will run when a request for the relevant URL is received. A gateway is typically a program that transforms information from one form to another, and one use for CGI scripts is to implement gateways. For example, you may have all your data in a relational database and want to make this information available to the Web. To do this you would write a gateway script to transform HTTP requests into accesses to your database and translate the replies into HTML.

Before CGI, each server passed the query information into a script in its own way. Unfortunately this made it difficult to write gateways that would work on more than one type of server, so a few of the server developers got together and CGI was the result. Some servers do not yet support CGI, but most of the popular ones do.

Writing CGI scripts

CGI passes the information a script needs into the script in environment variables. The most important two are:

- QUERY_STRING   The server will put the part of the URL after the first "?" in QUERY_STRING;
- PATH_INFO   The server will put the part of the path name after the scriptname in PATH_INFO.

For example, if we sent a request to the server with the URL:

http://www.cs.ucl.ac.uk/cgi-bin/htimage/usr/www/img/uk_map?404,451

and we had cgi-bin configured as a scripts directory, then the server would run the script called htimage. It would then pass the remaining path information /usr/www/img/uk_map to htimage in the PATH_INFO environment variable, and pass 404,451 in the QUERY_STRING variable. In this case, htimage is a script for implementing active maps supplied with the CERN HTTPD, and is described in more detail in Chapter 8.

The server expects the script program to produce some output on its standard output. It first expects to see a short MIME header, followed by a blank line, and then any other output the script wants returned to the client. The MIME header must have one or more of the following directives:

- Content-Type: *type/subtype*   This specifies the form of any output that follows.
- Location: *URL*   This specifies that the client should request the given URL rather than display the output. This is a redirection. Some servers may allow the URL to be a short URL, specifying only the file name and path; in this case the server will usually return the relevant file directly to the client, rather than sending a redirection.

The short MIME header can optionally contain a number of other MIME header fields. These will also be checked by the server, which will add any missing fields before passing the combined reply to the client.

Under some circumstances, the script may want to create the *entire* MIME header itself. For instance, you may want to do this if you want to specify expiry dates or status codes yourself, and do not need the server to parse your header and insert any missing fields. In this case, both the CERN and NCSA servers recognize scripts whose name begins nph- as having a "*no parse header*", and will not modify the reply at all. Under these circumstances your script will need access to extra information to be able to fill out all the header fields correctly, and so this information is also available via CGI environment variables.

The full list of CGI environment variables is:

- SERVER_SOFTWARE   This holds the name and version of the server that answered the request and is now running your script.

- SERVER_NAME   The server's hostname. This is useful if you need to generate URLs referring to this server in your script.

- GATEWAY_INTERFACE   The version of CGI that this server complies with. For example CGI/1.0.

- SERVER_PROTOCOL   The name and version of the protocol this request arrived with (i.e. the protocol the client speaks) For example, HTTP/1.0.

- SERVER_PORT   The port on the server that the request was sent to. Again, this is useful if you need to generate URLs referring to this server in your script.

- REQUEST_METHOD   The method of the request. For example, for HTTP, this might be GET, POST, HEAD, etc.

- PATH_INFO   The extra path information as given by the client. For example, sending a GET request to a server using the URL

  http://www.host/cgi-bin/htimage/usr/www/img/map1

  may cause the script htimage to be run from cgi-bin with PATH_INFO set to /usr/www/img/map1.

- PATH_TRANSLATED   This contains the data given in PATH_INFO after the server has attempted to translate it into a real path on your file system. The result may or may not be meaningful.

- SCRIPT_NAME   This is the virtual name and path of the script, as seen in a URL referencing it.

- QUERY_STRING   This contains the information contained after the "?" in the URL that caused this script to be executed. The information is just as it came from the URL, without having been URL decoded at all. This is used to hold the co-ordinate information in active maps, the text query with ISINDEX, the entire encoded form with forms that use the GET method and so on.

- REMOTE_HOST   The host name of the machine the client is running on. If the server does not know this, it should leave it unset and set REMOTE_ADDR instead.

- REMOTE_ADDR   The IP address of the machine the client is running on.

- **AUTH_TYPE** If the server supports user authentication and the script is protected, this is the authentication method that was used to validate the user's identity.

- **REMOTE_USER** If the server supports user authentication and the script is protected, this is the username the user gave to the authentication process.

- **REMOTE_IDENT** Some servers and client hosts support RFC 931 identification, whereby when the client connects to the server, the server queries the client's machine to find the username of the user who made the connection. This information is not always reliable and will reduce the performance of the server, but may be useful for some logging purposes.

- **CONTENT_TYPE** Queries such as PUT and POST (that can be used to submit forms) attach information to the body of the request. This is the MIME content type of the body of such a request.

- **CONTENT_LENGTH** This is the length of the attached information sent with a PUT or POST request.

A simple example of a CGI script written in the Bourne shell for a Unix system is:

```
#!/bin/sh
FINGER=`which finger`
echo Content-type: text/html
echo
if [ "$QUERY_STRING" = "" ]; then
    echo "<TITLE>Finger Gateway</TITLE>"
    echo "<H1>Finger Gateway</H1>"
    echo "<ISINDEX>"
    echo "This is a gateway to \"finger\". "
    echo "Type a user@host in your browser's search dialog.<P>"
else
    echo "<PRE>"
    $FINGER "$QUERY_STRING"
    echo "</PRE>"
fi
```

This generates a page of HTML allowing the user to enter the username of the person to query, unless it is called with a username in QUERY_STRING, in which case it executes the Unix finger command using QUERY_STRING as a parameter, and then returns the result to the user.

Active maps

One nice feature, which is now supported by most graphical WWW clients, is the ISMAP active map command, which can be associated with an HTML in-line image. This tells the WWW client to supply the x and y co-ordinates of the point the user clicks on within the image.

For example, this HTML tells the client this image is an active map:

```
<a href=/cgi-bin/imagemap/uk_map>
    <img src=uk_map_lbl.gif ISMAP>
</a>
```

When the user clicks on the map at, say, point (404,451), her client will submit a GET request to the server:

```
GET /cgi-bin/imagemap/uk_map?404.451 HTTP/1.0
```

For this to do anything interesting, the server must interpret

```
/cgi-bin/imagemap/uk_map
```

as something special – a server script to be executed rather than a file to be retrieved. How the server decides that this is a command depends on the type of server. As an example, NCSA's HTTPD allows the directory cgi-bin to be defined as a script alias. MacHTTP allows you to configure filename extensions such as .script to denote executable scripts. However, whichever server you run, the 404.451 part will then be passed to the command as parameters.

When the server script is executed, it could generate output that is to be returned directly to the client – for instance, the command could generate HTML directly as output. However the usual way imagemaps are used is to access other existing pages of HTML using HTTP redirection. This is where the server first returns to the client the URL of the place to look for the page corresponding to the place they clicked on the map, and then the client goes and requests this new URL (usually without bothering to ask the user).

We look at how to configure active maps for a few servers in Chapter 8.

Forms

Forms are one way the World Wide Web allows users to submit information to servers. All the mechanisms described so far allow users to choose from a set of available options. Forms let users type information into their Web browser and then get the server to run a program with their submission as input. Examples of things you might type are keys to search a database (e.g. what films was Zazu Pits in?).

Laying out forms

HTML provides a number of commands for telling the client to do something special. The first command is FORM which tells the client that everything between one <FORM> command and the next </FORM> terminator is part of the same form. The form command can take a number of attributes:

- ACTION=http://www.host.name/cgi-bin/query   This gives the URL of the script to run when the form is submitted. You must supply an ACTION attribute with the FORM command.
- METHOD=GET   This is the default method for submitting a form. The contents of the form will be added to the end of the URL that is sent to the server.
- METHOD=POST   The post method causes the information contained in the form to be sent to the server in the body of the request.
- ENCTYPE=application/x-www-form-urlencoded   This specifies how the information the user typed into the form should be encoded. Currently only the default, application/x-www-form-urlencoded, is allowed.

If your server supports the POST method, it is advisable to use it, as if you use the GET method, it is possible that long forms will be truncated when they are passed from the server to the script.

The INPUT command

Now you have an empty form, you probably want to provide some boxes and buttons that the user can set. These are created using the INPUT tag. This is used in a similar way to the IMG tag for images – there's no need for a terminating tag as it does not surround anything. There are several types of INPUT tag, denoted by the TYPE attribute:

- <INPUT TYPE=text NAME=users_name>   This is a simple text entry field that we have called users_name. The user never sees this NAME attribute displayed on her client – it is purely so that we can keep track of which field is which when we come to process the form. Text entries also allow you to specify:
  - VALUE="enter your name here"   This lets you specify the default text to appear in the entry box.
  - SIZE=60,3   This lets you specify the size of the entry box in characters. For example the above says the entry box should be 60 characters wide and three lines high.
  - MAXLENGTH=8   This lets you specify the maximum number of characters you will allow to be entered in a single line text entry box. For instance, you might only allow a user to enter eight characters as their user name.
- <INPUT TYPE=password NAME=users_passwd>   This is also a text entry

79

field, but the characters the user types are displayed as stars so that other people cannot read the password from the screen. Password fields also support the VALUE, SIZE and MAXLENGTH attributes.

- <INPUT TYPE=checkbox NAME=veggie>   This is a single button that is either on or off. Checkboxes also support the following attributes:
  - VALUE="true"   This is the value to return if the checkbox is set to "on". If it's set to "off", no value is returned.
  - CHECKED   This says that the checkbox is "on" by default.

- <INPUT TYPE=radio NAME=food_style VALUE=indian>
  <INPUT TYPE=radio NAME=food_style VALUE=chinese>
  These are a collection of buttons. Radio buttons with the same name are grouped together so that selecting one of them turns the others off like the channel tuning buttons on some radios. Radio buttons also support the VALUE and CHECKED attributes, but only one radio button can be specified as CHECKED.

- <INPUT TYPE=submit VALUE="Press Me to Submit">   This is a button that submits the contents of the form to the server using the method in the surrounding FORM. Submit buttons do not have a NAME attribute, but you can specify the label for the button using a VALUE attribute.

- <INPUT TYPE=reset VALUE="Press Me to Start Again">   This is a button that causes the various boxes and buttons in the form to reset to their default values. Reset buttons also do not have a NAME attribute, but allow a VALUE attribute to label the button.

The SELECT command

If you want to provide the user with a long list of items to choose from, it is not very natural to use radio buttons, so HTML provides another command – SELECT. Unlike INPUT, this does have a closing </SELECT> tag. Each option within the list is denoted using the <OPTION> tag. Options must be plain text – no embedded HTML commands are allowed:

```
<SELECT NAME="food style">
<OPTION> Chinese
<OPTION> South Indian
<OPTION> North Indian
<OPTION> Greek
</SELECT>
```

SELECT must have a NAME attribute, and also allows the following attributes:
- SIZE=3   This says how many of the options are visible at once, in this case, three.

80

- MULTIPLE   This allows the user to select more than one item from the list. The default is that only one item can be selected at once.

OPTION tags can also have a SELECTED attribute that says that this option is selected by default. If the SELECT command has a MULTIPLE attribute, then several OPTION tags are allowed to be pre-selected in this way.

The TEXTAREA command

If you want to allow the user to enter a large amount of text, you could use an <INPUT TYPE=text> tag, but HTML also provides another command – TEXTAREA. TEXTAREA fields automatically have scroll bars on Mosaic and any amount of text can be entered into them.

TEXTAREA fields must have a NAME attribute, and also must have ROWS and COLS attributes specifying how large the visible area of the TEXTAREA is in characters. TEXTAREA fields, like SELECT fields must have a closing tag:

```
<TEXTAREA NAME="address" ROWS=4 COLS=60>
Any default contents go here
</TEXTAREA>
```

The default contents must be ordinary text with no HTML formatting commands.

An example form

An example of a form that demonstrates many of these features is:

```
<HEAD><TITLE>Pub List Feedback</TITLE></HEAD>
<BODY>
<H1>Pub List Feedback</H1>
Please use this form to let us know about any good pubs you come
across in London.
<FORM ACTION=http://www.cs.ucl.ac.uk/cgi-bin/pubform METHOD=POST>
<HR>
<B>Pub Name:</B>
<INPUT TYPE=text NAME=pubname SIZE=40>
<P>
<B>Pub Address:</B>
<INPUT TYPE=text NAME=pubaddress SIZE=40,4>
<P>
<B>Area of London:</B>
<SELECT NAME=area SIZE=4>
<OPTION SELECTED>Bloomsbury
<OPTION>Theatreland
```

```
<OPTION>The City
<OPTION>Kensington and Chelsea
<OPTION>Out of the Centre
<OPTION>Further afield
</SELECT>
<HR>
<TEXTAREA NAME=description ROWS=6 COLS=80>Describe your pub here!
</TEXTAREA>
<p>
<INPUT TYPE=radio NAME=grade VALUE=1>Average.
<INPUT TYPE=radio NAME=grade VALUE=2 CHECKED>Worth going to.
<INPUT TYPE=radio NAME=grade VALUE=3>Worth a detour.
<INPUT TYPE=radio NAME=grade VALUE=4>Worth a long detour!
<HR>
<B>Your Name:</B>
<INPUT TYPE=text NAME=username SIZE=40>
<P>
<B>Your email address:</B>
<INPUT TYPE=text NAME=useremail SIZE=40>
<P>
<I>(You can leave these blank if you don't want to be credited)</I>
<hr>
<INPUT TYPE=submit VALUE="I've finished now">
<INPUT TYPE=reset VALUE="Ooops, can I start again?">
</FORM>
</BODY>
```

See Figure 5.9 for how this looks on the NCSA Mosaic browser.

Submitting forms to the server

As we mentioned above, there are two ways you can submit a form to a server – the GET method and the POST method. These methods refer to the type of request the browser makes to the client.

GET is the normal way a browser requests a page or an image from a server; the URL gives the location of the file we want or the name of the script that will produce the data we want. We saw with imagemaps that we could also send a small amount of additional data to a script in the URL by putting it at the end of the URL after a question mark. You can also send all the information contained in your form to the server in the same way. However, it is possible that some servers may have size limits in the amount of data they can pass to the script in this way.

POST is an entirely different method from those we have seen so far. A POST

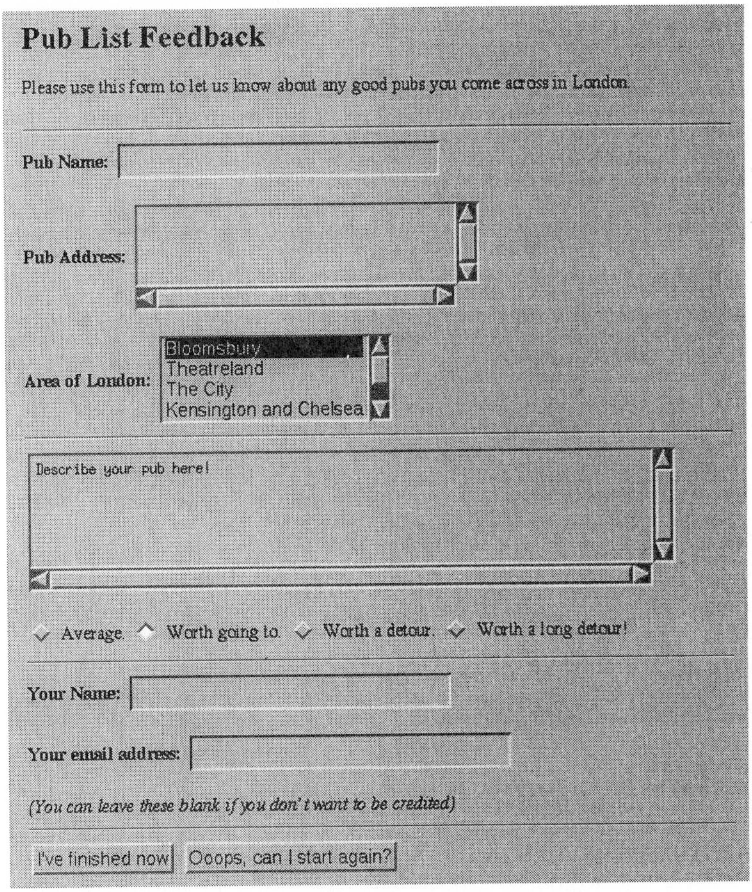

Figure 5.9 An example form as displayed by NCSA Mosaic.

request consists of a URL that refers to the script we wish to run, and then a URL encoded body that contains the data from our form. URL encoding replaces spaces with "+" and encodes other special characters as "%XX" where XX is the ASCII code for the character in octal.

If your server supports the POST method, we recommend that you use it – using the GET method may work, but if your forms are large, it is really stretching the intended purpose of GET somewhat.

Doing something with the form

Like active maps, handling of forms differs somewhat from server to server. We discuss this in detail for the main servers in Chapter 8.

Where are we now?

Now you know in some detail how clients and servers work. There is a great deal more to learn, but it is mainly concerned with local system-specific details. The basics are all here.

There are regular new releases of servers and new tools become available all the time. If you have a problem, or need a new tool, the chances are that some-one else has had the same need and, if you are lucky, someone has already solved the problem. Check the online documentation about the server you are using, and do not forget that CGI programs from one server should work on another.

Chapter 6

Academic examples of WWW servers

For this chapter, we unashamedly chose an academic example, our own server, which can be found at `http://www.cs.ucl.ac.uk/`.

For political, historical and natural reasons, we also have a quick look at the UK's Open Government server run by the CCTA at `http://www.open.gov.uk/`, the Natural History Museum, at `http://www.nhm.ac.uk/` and the Royal Horticultural Society's server at Kew, at `http://www.rbgkew.org.uk/`.

The extended example shown is the attempt to set up a coherent WWW service for the educational needs of the authors' department (the Department of Computer Science, University College London, or UCL CS). We use this to illustrate several points. First, schools and universities make their income primarily from the business of teaching. Hence, advertising what they do effectively using WWW (and any other cost/effective means available) is essential to reach potential students. Secondly, universities conduct basic research, which is usually pre-competitive, and it is therefore in the public's strong interest for that research to be made as available as possible. In fact, in the UK, universities are assessed and partly funded on the basis of their publication records. Lastly, the WWW can be used as a single source for co-ordinating administrative information, keeping inaccurate or out-of-date copies to a minimum, and saving immense amounts of paper. Socially, access to information about education can only be an advantage.

A key fact to remember about an academic community is that it is very hard to impose a single word-processing standard on its members. In these examples, source material was prepared using packages as diverse as FrameMaker, WordPerfect, Nroff, LaTeX and MacDraw.

The following notes on style and maintenance may be useful:

- Avoid: *information about blah is stored HERE* Rather, use: *We also have information about BLAH*

- Avoid (large or any) GIFs in home pages. Most people are on the end of slow lines, and will be for a couple more years.

85

- Timely information, e.g. program schedules, needs a regular process of transfer (and update) from printed/WP publication to and from WWW. This takes a lot of (worthwhile) initial effort, which should not be underestimated. Put in place a life cycle for bringing online new information, and for *garbage collecting* what is out of date. Think about the hypertext structure when you consider the organizational structure of this life cycle.

Syllabuses/course administration

A university course has a lot of intertwined administration, much of which can be accessed in many contexts. UCL CS has a number of undergraduate and postgraduate courses made up of modules, with various possible options. In addition, some of these options can be taken in different years. The department also publishes booklets about its courses, which contain more global information about the college and the views of students. The syllabuses can be referenced from the timetable information. This is accessed by students and staff to find where they should be and when. Examination information may also be linked in and so on. The easiest way to express all this linkage is through a hypertext web. The use of WWW also allows each owner of a course to control its source and update it asynchronously (i.e. not all at the start of term – or two weeks later, as is often, lamentably, the case).

Roles, such as timetabler or examiner, can be changed and easily learned without exchange of large amounts of expertise that can now be embedded in the links in the web. Some of this can be seen in Figure 6.1.

Brochures, syllabuses, etc. and a searchable project list, as well as options and timetables can easily be converted for storage in your server, as in Figure 6.2. A natural extension might be to provide timetables via a CGI back end, to allow searches for person, room, course, etc.

Course notes

Going one stage further, we can store in the Web, under the syllabuses, the entire notes (as in Figure 6.3) for a course. This has several advantages over traditional technology. New lecturers and students perceive the structure and the proportion a course has. New courses can be formed by dissecting and sewing together old ones as obsolescence creeps in. Linkages between courses and staff interests (prerequisites, follow-on courses, etc.) can be made clear.

Some courses, for example projects, involve supervisors. Typically, supervisors suggest projects by putting their suggestions in their Web pages and then the syllabus page for projects can simply be a collection of links to the places within their pages where these suggestions are:

```
<UL>
 . . .
<LI> <A HREF=jon.html\#project>Jon's Project Suggestions</A>
```

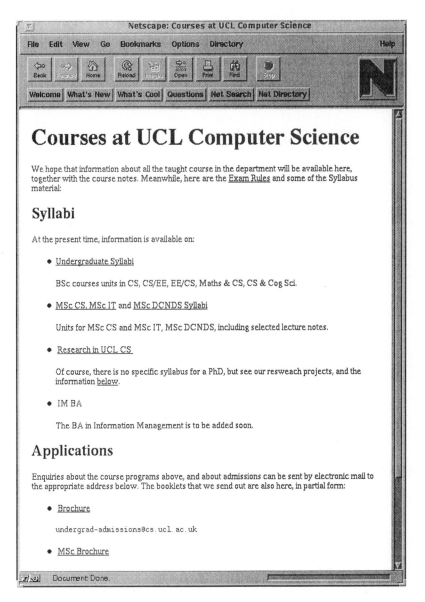

Figure 6.1   Course administration.

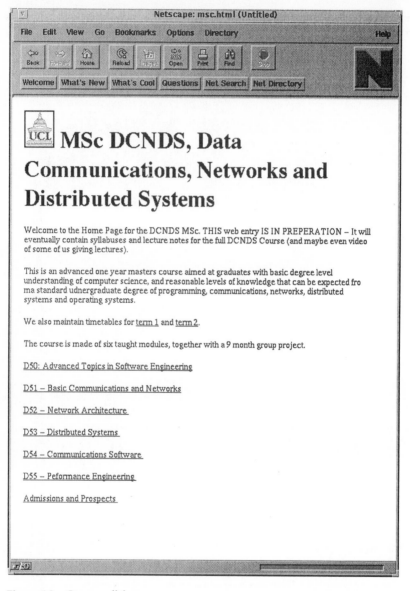

Figure 6.2   Course syllabuses.

Filters and links

As has been said, there are a number of filters that convert from native word-processor input, or output, to HTML. This means that we do not have to force a "house style" on course authors when they write the material. We get the

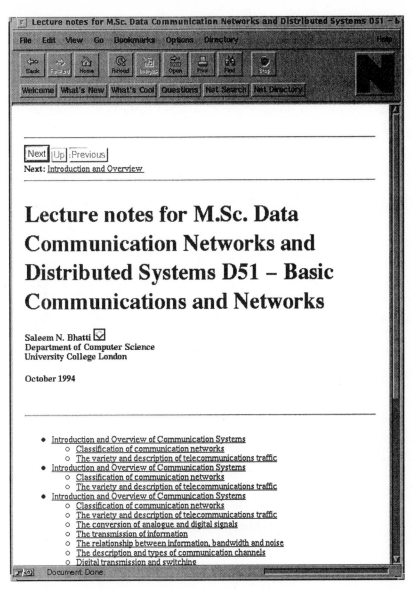

Figure 6.3   Course notes.

house style that the reader's WWW client program is configured for. This also obviates the learning of a new package by authors.

One interesting problem with letting people author their material in many different systems is that of maintaining links. Each word-processing package has its own idea of references, citations or bibliographies. Indeed, some systems even have hypertext built in nowadays, but of their own design. We would like to make sure that URLs can be associated with similar kinds of logical links in original source documents, e.g. references/citations in papers, course notes (to papers, books (ISBNs), other courses, etc.). Depending on the filter, it may be possible to translate these into URLs appropriately.

On the other hand, it may be necessary to persuade people to start to use different ways of specifying links in the package they are using, so that the

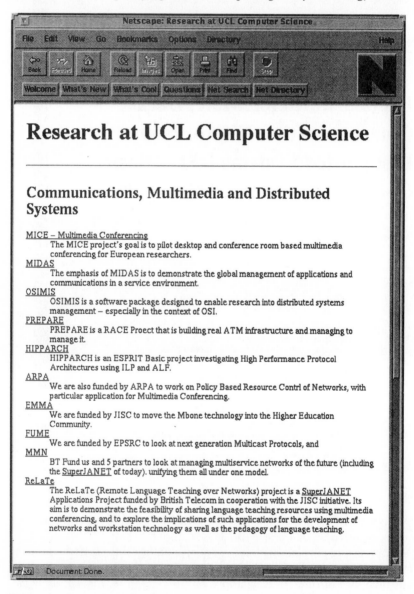

Figure 6.4   Research top level.

filter for that package can translate these correctly into URLs. This latter approach is used, for example in the excellent latex2html tool from Nikos Drakos at Leeds University in the UK. Filters that are in common use include:

- **latex2html** Deals with LaTeX to HTML. You can annotate your LaTeX source so that references in LaTeX form become links in HTML – this is ideal for developing course material that is structured.

- **fm2html and WebMaker** Deal with FrameMaker conversion to HTML.

- **groff2html** Converts groff to HTML.

- **ms2html** Converts nroff with MS macros to HTML

- **mm2html** As ms2html, but with MM macros – we had to roll our own, just to see how easy it was.

- **rtf2html** *and* **rtftohtml** Convert RTF (Rich Text Format), which is the most common intermediate form for PC and Macintosh word-processing packages. This is, unfortunately, operating at a level below that where one can extract true document structure, so is not generally as successful as tools that convert from document source forms.

There are also many useful ancillary tools (*pstogif*) for converting pictures from one bitmap format to another.

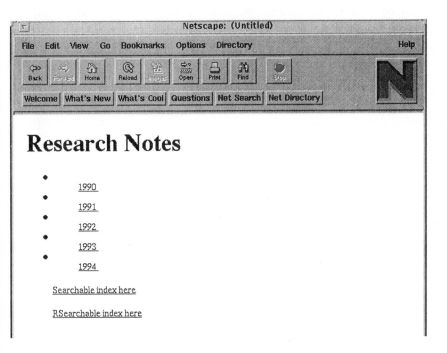

Figure 6.5   Research publications.

Research publications

A university lives partly by its teaching and partly by its research. Some of our research can be seen in Figure 6.4.

A university's research must be published (at least that is still the expectation in this decade). Often, finding one's way through the maze of publica-

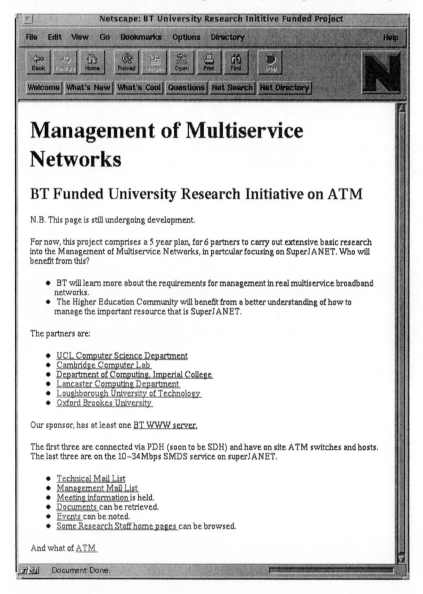

Figure 6.6   Example of collaboration pages – all links.

tions to the current hot topics and hot places is fraught with dead ends and so on. Research is often in a global context, and the Web as a way of publishing work in progress and placing it in context is very powerful.

However, we can also provide a very simple and useful function: searching and ordering of old reports – the cost of OCR (optical character recognition) and storing these on line may be prohibitive, but the cost of storing titles and

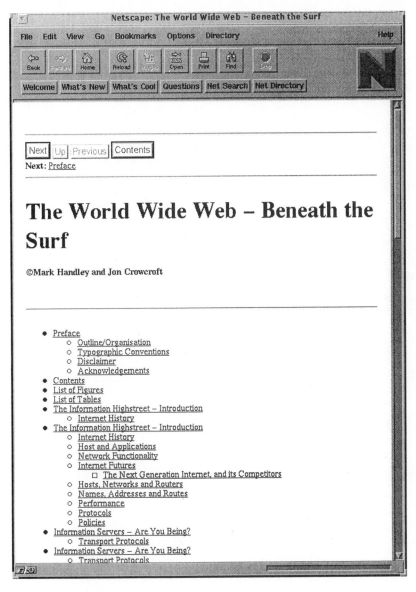

Figure 6.7   Beneath the surf.

abstracts going back several decades may be very small. An interface to this is shown in Figure 6.5.

To provide indexing and searching, the most common trick is to use the WAIS index and search programs. The results are then accessed via CGI, as described in Chapter 5.

Co-ordination of research projects

Projects are often collaborative – staff come and go and research directions change. The linkages between research organizations can be made explicit by including the partners' Web servers in a project home page, as shown for one of our larger projects in Figure 6.6.

Figure 6.8 Government.

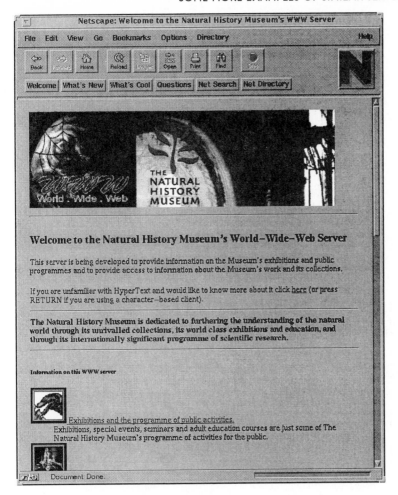

Figure 6.9   The Natural History Museum.

Some more examples of similar server sites

It will not be long before you can find books like this one on the Web (Fig. 6.7). And of course, governments are keen to prove they are keeping up with the times, as are historians and, naturally, botanists, as shown in Figures 6.8, 6.9 and 6.10.

Government agencies often spend a great deal in disseminating information through the media and through their own publishing organizations. For example, health and safety information and educational information, as well as general policy, need to be widely distributed. Online information services (see Fig. 6.8) allow those concerned with and about such policies to browse them at leisure, and to provide feedback, while maintaining relevance and focus.

95

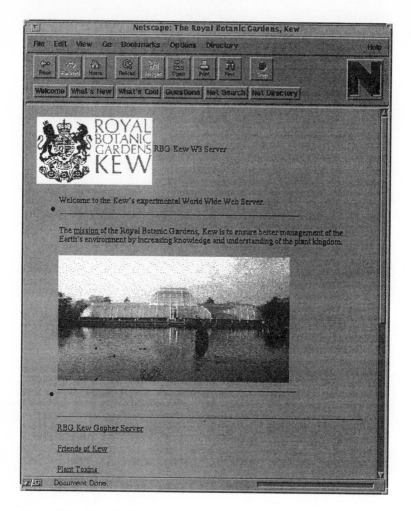

Figure 6.10   Kew Gardens.

Museums and botanical gardens are public services in the UK. They are often undersubscribed, simply through lack of public awareness. Just as with commercial services (see the next chapter), it is in the interest of those providing the service to maximize public knowledge of exactly what is on offer (Figs 6.9, 6.10).

Chapter 7
Commercial Web servers

Any statement we make about the number of commercial servers on the Web would be out of date in next to no time. At the time of writing, the majority are high-technology companies describing computing and network related services, but this is already beginning to change.

As the users of the Internet become more broadly based, the number of interesting non-computing Web servers is increasing rapidly. We present a couple of such servers that have already proved successful.

In this chapter, we look at the way that three organizations use the World Wide Web. The first is a trading company that is able to use electronic information and networking to replace almost completely real offices and resources. This has clear benefits in material costs. The information they provide is about items for sale or purchase and, in particular, benefits from graphical detail.

The second example is a media company, and specifically the television side of the company. A large organization like this has to deal with scale through hierarchical organization of its information. This is visible in the BBC's Web Server pages, as well as in the value of timely, international low, or zero, cost availability of public information about its works. Timeliness, here, is of the essence.

Newspapers provide digested information with editorial commentary, but typically take a while to go to press. Using the Web (with no loss of the visual impact of pictures) gives a newspaper something of the immediacy of television, but with the traditional quality control of content.

In all three cases, there is some benefit, no doubt, from being early to use this technology. International access is clearly of general value, as is fast turn-around. This advantage is also a disadvantage to organizations whose virtual goods are largely graphical, since in current networks, the further one wishes to disseminate information, the slower the networks are.

As in Chapter 6, we use extensive examples to show that the complete range of business can be captured in an organization's pages.

Carl Philips Yachting

Carl Philips Yachting is a yacht brokerage in Hampshire, England. Its business is buying and selling yachts – by its nature this is an international business that fits well with the international nature of the Web.

As you would expect with a small business such as this, it does not run its own server, but instead rents space on the Web server of the local commercial Internet provider – Aladdin Internet.

By comparison with some, the server is relatively simple, with a listing of some of the yachts available and then detailed information and pictures of each yacht.

Carl Philips Yachting makes good use of pictures of each yacht or of a yacht of the same type and feature plans of many (Figs 7.1–7.4).

To print this information in colour and send plans out to prospective buyers takes time and costs money. The Web has no reproduction cost, very little distribution cost and much larger (if less focused) coverage that any yachting magazine. The costs involved in maintaining the server are minimal, given

Figure 7.1   Carl Philips Yachting home page.

Yachts for Sale

Sailing Yachts

- Alchemy g – an immaculate no expense spared luxury cruising yacht by Ron Holland, over 67 feet of quality workmanship and design – only $795,000.
- Jos of Hamble – an X–382 from Denmark for £120,000 – Immaculate Condition
- Sharp Exit – an IMX 38 Racer/Cruiser for £96,000 – only one year old!
- Xpro – an IMX 38 Racer/Cruiser for £89,750 – winning pedigree!
- Sir Vagabond – a Sigma 46 for only £55,000 ex vat
- Eric the X Boat – an X–342 Cruiser Racer for £47,750
- Eau De Vie – a superb example of an X 342 Cruiser Racer for £45,000.
- Magda – an MG 335 Fin keel Cruiser Racer for £39,750
- Xpedite – an X–99 optimised for racing at £32,500
- Reaction II – a Contessa 33 in smart condition at £27,750
- Drazue – Moody 27 Cruiser for £23,500
- Reverie Of Gosport – A Gib'Sea 84 with extensive inventory for £19,750
- Swift – a Hunter 26 Bilge keel Cruiser for only £15,750
- Papillon – a Dufour 2800 for £15,750
- Mabrook – a Westerly Centaur Bilge Keel Cruiser for £14,750
- Blondie – A David Thomas Boleso for only £6,950

Figure 7.2   Yachts for sale.

File   Edit   View   Go   Bookmarks   Options   Directory   Help

Back   Forward   Home   Reload   Images   Open   Print   Find   Stop

Location: http://beta.aladdin.co.uk/cpy/srvagbnd.html

Particulars of SIGMA 41 Cruiser/Racer Fin Keel –

SIR VAGABOND

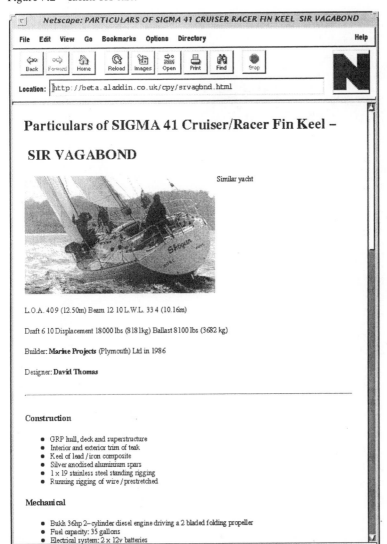

Similar yacht

L.O.A. 40 9 (12.50m) Beam 12 10 L.W.L. 33 4 (10.16m)

Draft 6 10 Displacement 18000 lbs (8181kg) Ballast 8100 lbs (3682 kg)

Builder: **Marine Projects** (Plymouth) Ltd in 1986

Designer: **David Thomas**

Construction

- GRP hull, deck and superstructure
- Interior and exterior trim of teak
- Keel of lead / iron composite
- Silver anodised aluminium spars
- 1 x 19 stainless steel standing rigging
- Running rigging of wire / prestretched

Mechanical

- Bukh 36hp 2–cylinder diesel engine driving a 2 bladed folding propeller
- Fuel capacity: 35 gallons
- Electrical system: 2 x 12v batteries

Document: Done.

Figure 7.3   Particulars of a yacht.

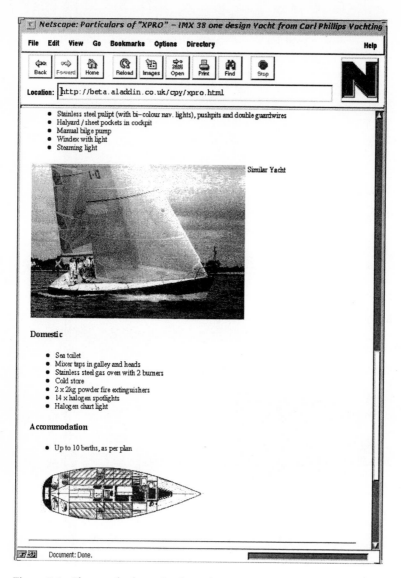

Figure 7.4   Photo and schematic of a yacht.

that the company needs to keep the details of the yachts online anyway to print the paper equivalent.

Although this is the first online yacht brokerage in the UK, it is not likely to be the last, as the company reports a quite a number of enquiries from all over the world as a result.

Mass media in the Web

An enterprise can use the network to carry information that increases the visibility of its other services. For example, any publishing company, whatever media it works with, can benefit from exposure of its works. In the rest of this chapter, we take a look at two such enterprises, the BBC and the *Daily Telegraph*. What characterizes these services is that they are providing information that will increase the take up of other services (e.g. watching TV stations and reading the newspaper), but require no element of charging for what they do make visible.

A major television company's server

The BBC has a history of innovation in technology, as well as involvement in education (via the world's first online university, the Open University). Not

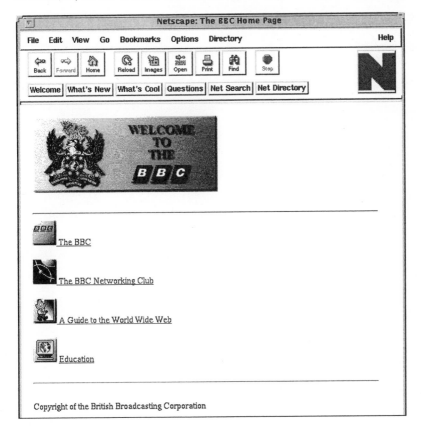

Figure 7.5   The BBC's top page.

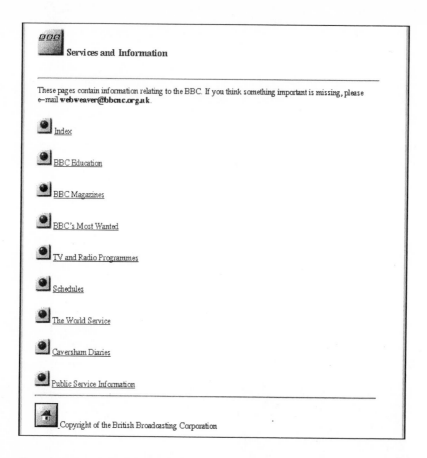

Figure 7.6   BBC Information Services.

surprisingly, the BBC has an excellent WWW server, to be found at

`http://www.bbcnc.org.uk/.`

The BBC broadcasts world wide, as well as selling its television and radio programmes, and ancillary books, to other agencies around the world. Thus use of the world-wide Internet and WWW to disseminate information about these services provides very valuable exposure.

The home page shown in Figure 7.5 has a limited number of GIFs, as many of its clients will be accessing it over dial-up lines. It is a clear index to the rest of the BBC service, as well as containing an identifying logo, which is visible on most of the authored pages. The BBC's online services are then listed on the next page, Figure 7.6.

A TV company also publishes in other media. The BBC publishes quite a few books and magazines to complement its television and radio programmes. For

Figure 7.7   *Top Gear* magazine's front page.

 Full Metal Racket audio tape

Sixteen of the world's finest engines in a classic concerto of combustion. The might and majesty of motoring mechanicals, laid bare by the artistry of digital recording. Marvel at inlet roar and turbo howl as we rev 16 of the world's finest engines. Please make sure that before you download any of the sound files you have the necessary software to play them.

A few clips to wet your whistle with.

1. 1962 Ferrari GTO V12 with voice-over (Sun audio format 204k)

2. 1930 4.5-litre Bentley – sound only (Sun audio format 174k)

3. 1935 Aston Martin Ulster – sound only (Sun audio format 129k)

4. 1955 D-Type Jaguar with voice-over (Sun audio format 287k)

If you'd like your very own copy of this very noisy tape, here's what to do:

ACCESS, VISA and MASTERCARD orders accepted by phone and fax:

Order by phone (10:00 to 15:00 GMT): (+44) 0 1937 541067 By fax: (+44) 0 1937 845381

How much? All prices in GBP's. UK/Europe orders 3.99 plus 1.00 post and pack – total 5.24
North America and Canada 6.00
Rest of the world 6.50
Hint: Play side two very loudly with the windows open when you're stuck in traffic.

Figure 7.8   Sounds of cars on the Web.

Programme Schedules

Monday, January 23, 1995

7.00

THE ADVENTURES OF BUZZY BEE AND FRIENDS (Nicam Digital Stereo)

A series of country tales for younger viewers based on the popular books by Paule Alen, Myriam Deru and Erw
discover the mysteries of nature. Buzzy Bee decides to help a baby cuckoo bird find a home. (Repeat)

7.05

THE FAMILY NESS

Cartoon adventures of a family of monsters who live in Loch Ness, and their two friends Elspeth and Angus. (Re

7.10

THE LEGEND OF PRINCE VALIANT (Ceefax) (Nicam Digital Stereo)

The adventures of a daring young Viking prince, searching for the magical castle of Camelot. (Repeat)

7.35

WHITE FANG

The story of a half wolf, half husky and his relationship with a seventeen–year–old boy, Matt, and set in the Roc
McIlwraith, Denise Virieux.

8.00

BREAKFAST NEWS (Ceefax) (Sign language and subtitles)

Figure 7.9   BBC 5 TV and Radio top level.

 BBC Television programmes categorised by type

- business programmes
- cookery programmes
- education programmes
- films
- children's programmes
- music & arts
- news programmes
- science programmes
- sports programmes
- transport programmes
- travel programmes

Figure 7.10   BBC programmes categorized by type.

example, there are cookery books and children's story books, as well as transcripts of the programmes themselves. Figure 7.7 shows a page about a magazine that accompanies the programmes about cars and driving, which illustrates the use of graphics and audio to good effect. As part of a driving interest, the online version allows you to retrieve the sound of some loud and fast cars in action, as shown in Figure 7.8.

Of course, the BBC's main business is broadcasting. It has information about what programmes are on its radio and TV stations world wide, and even transcripts of some of the programmes in the following pages, as can be seen in Figures 7.9 and 7.10. The latter shows the advantage of online information over print – it can be presented in a variety of ways, so that you can retrieve the programme listings by subject or by time.

The BBC operates worldwide, which means that it spans many time zones. In Figure 7.11 the footprint of a satellite for world service TV over Africa is shown. There are also pages that allow you to search maps for programme times and frequencies.

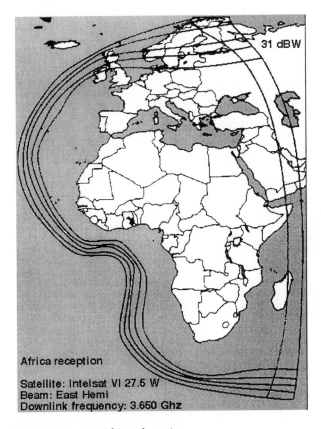

Figure 7.11 BBC African footprint.

?BBC Key Corporate Dates

Some key corporate dates 1922 – 1991

1922

18 Oct British Broadcasting Company Ltd formed
1 Nov Broadcasting Licence Fee of 10 shillings introduced
14 Nov Firstly daily transmission from 2LO
15 Nov First broadcasts from Birmingham and Manchester
14 Dec John Reith made General Manager of BBC
23 Dec First orchestral concert, regular general news bulletin from London, talk and dance music
24 Dec First play written for radio and first religious address

1923

8 Jan First outside broadcast
18 Jan Licence from Postmaster–General issued to British Broadcasting Company Ltd
30 Jan First variety programme
17 Feb First broadcast appeal
22 Feb First broadcast debate
26 Mar First daily weather forecast
29 Apr First SOS message
2 May First afternoon talk for women
28 May First full–length play
29 Aug First simultaneous broadcast of news over all stations
28 Sept Radio Times first published
8 Nov First broadcast in Welsh from Cardiff
26 Nov First experimental broadcast to America
2 Dec First broadcast in Gaelic from Aberdeen
30 Dec First continental programme relayed by landline

1924

6 Jan First religious service
5 Feb First Greenwich Time Signal
17 Feb First Big Ben daily time signal
4 Apr First national schools broadcast
23 Apr First broadcast by King George V
12 Jun First disc–jockey programme
13 Oct First broadcast election address (by the Prime Minister, Ramsay MacDonald)
10 Nov First running commentary (Lord Mayor's Show)
26 Nov First relay from America

1925

19 Feb First broadcast for farmers (market prices)

1926

Figure 7.12   BBC history.

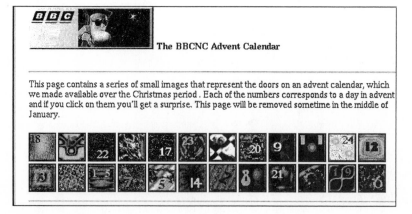

The BBCNC Advent Calendar

This page contains a series of small images that represent the doors on an advent calendar, which we made available over the Christmas period. Each of the numbers corresponds to a day in advent and if you click on them you'll get a surprise. This page will be removed sometime in the middle of January.

Figure 7.13   The BBC's 1994 Advent calendar.

Figure 7.14   A history of Santa Claus.

Any large corporation needs to educate customers and new employees about its history – some of the BBC's can be seen in Figure 7.12.

The BBC operates a networking club. One of the most imaginative things this was used for in 1994 was an Advent Calendar. In Figure 7.13, you can see the calendar. Each GIF for a day is actually a pointer to further information. For example, Figure 7.14 shows a history of Santa Claus that someone else on the network provided. As the Marx brothers said, "there ain't no Sanity Clause".

A major newspaper's server

The *Daily Telegraph* is one of England's foremost quality newspapers. It was also the first to provide the entire paper online (at least up until *yesterday's edition*). It is at http://www.telegraph.co.uk/, as shown in Figure 7.15.

The first thing that you find here is that the designers have thought about possible future access control. Once you have registered, you will be given (and emailed) a PIN (personal identification number, just like the one you

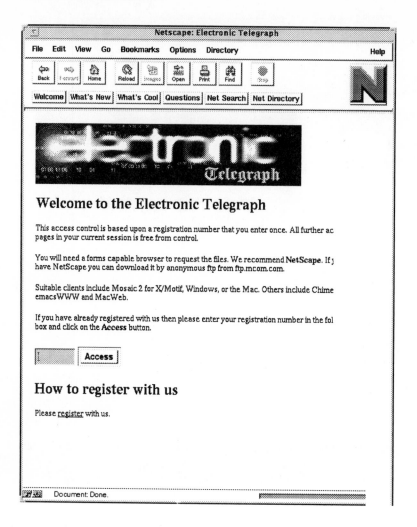

Figure 7.15   The *Electronic Telegraph*.

might use to access a cash machine). At a future stage, it is clear that the *Telegraph* could contact users via some secure mechanism (letter, fax, telephone, or anything adequately covered by law) and establish a charging mechanism. This could simply involve direct debit or standing order or be any standard means of charging. While a user remains in credit with the provider, their PIN remains valid. If a user stops paying, the PIN can be withdrawn. There might be some concern over interlopers wire tapping and seizing a legitimate PIN and misusing it. This could easily be prevented by the use of *one-time passwords*. These are changed each time the user uses the service. If a user finds that the next password they have been given fails, they contact the service

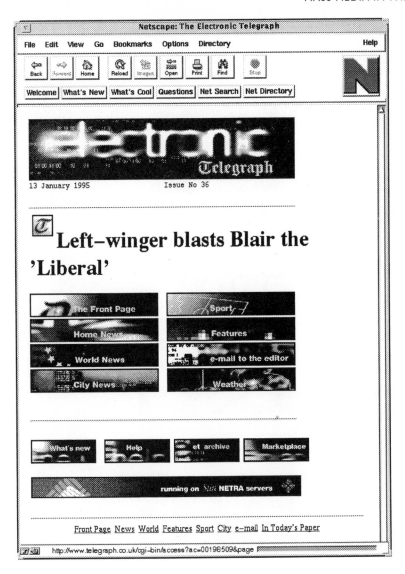

Figure 7.16   The *Electronic Telegraph* today.

provider and complain; they can then be issued with a new unique starting identity, thus minimizing the value of intrusions. We discuss further security mechanisms in the final chapter of the book.

Once you have registered, you can proceed to the real top page, as shown in Figure 7.16. This, as can be seen, is a graphical and text index of the rest of the edition. Note that, although there are a lot of graphics here, the bottom of the page is a text-only menu, which is nicely designed for Lynx access. The large number of graphical items may overload even links with quite reasonable

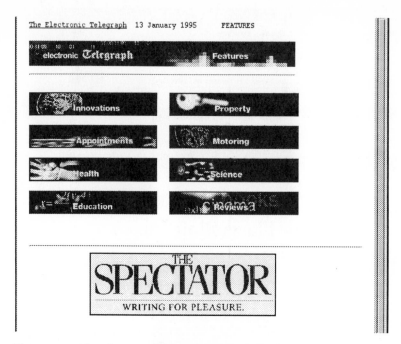

Figure 7.17   The *Electronic Telegraph's* Features top page.

Figure 7.18   Holiday places in Spain.

speed access. However, since the *Telegraph* was the first quality national on the net, we believe that it has gained more kudos by having a well designed service. Later refinements may entail reducing the size and quantity of images (on the other hand, networks will get faster).

The features page (Fig. 7.17) again contains graphics and pointers to the actual contents. Below this are pages with text and photographs like that in Figure 7.18, for example. It would be quite simple to provide onward links from these to related information from other servers – for example, a holiday

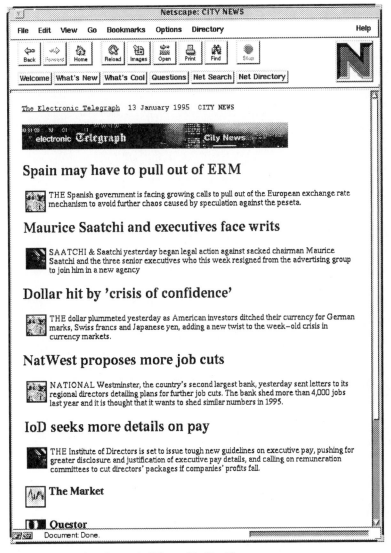

Figure 7.19 The *Electronic Telegraph's* City News top page.

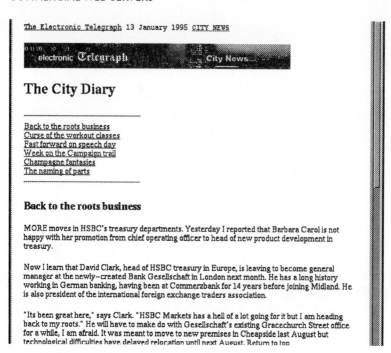

Figure 7.20   The *Electronic Telegraph's* City Diary.

page could be linked to the region's weather server.

The City of London is a major economic centre. All quality dailies carry City news, and here in Figures 7.19 and 7.20 we can see the City News top page and the City Diary.

It is not enough to enter the electronic world simply as a broadcaster or disseminator of information. The Internet is interactive, and all good servers make use of this. Most newspapers have a page for letters to the editor. The *Electronic Telegraph* is no different. Figure 7.21 shows the page for email to the Editor.

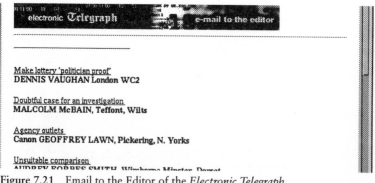

Figure 7.21   Email to the Editor of the *Electronic Telegraph*.

Figure 7.22   Home news on the *Electronic Telegraph*.

The *Telegraph* carries home and sports news (Figs 7.22, 7.23, 7.24) and over a period of time, such an online resource could build up to replace special-purpose publications such as almanacs, with a more rapidly searchable facility that could end arguments about famous results or act as an *aide memoire*.

Finally, newspaper photographers are famous for their still images of important moments in time, either for the world or for an individual. You will have to guess which event Figure 7.25 represents.

England unable to force way into Australia's private party

WELL, it was not an inglorious failure, but the fact is that, needing 237 runs minimum to reach the finals of the World Series Cup, England could not manage it more

Mandela Trophy: S African openers in record form

SOUTH AFRICA will take a psychological advantage into next week's one-off Test against Pakistan at the Wanderers after thrashing them by 157 runs in taking the Mandela Trophy with a match to spare. more

Figure 7.23   Cricket on the *Electronic Telegraph*.

Fall of wickets: 1–11, 2–46, 3–207, 4–245, 5–262.

Did Not Bat: M G Hughes, P E McIntyre, P R Reiffel, S P George.

Bowling: Fraser 10–1–36–0; DeFreitas 10–2–43–1; Lewis 6–0–48–2; Udal 10–0–56–2; Hick 8–0–40–0; Gooch 6–0–34–0.

ENGLAND

```
G A Gooch c Emery b Hughes          17
*M A Atherton c Emery b Reiffel     20
G A Hick b McIntyre                 35
G P Thorpe c Reiffel b McIntyre     24
J P Crawley c Emery b George        37
M W Gatting lbw b Hughes            15
-S J Rhodes c George b McIntyre     23
C C Lewis not out                   22
P A J DeFreitas b Blewett           12
S D Udal lbw b Reiffel               9
A R C Fraser not out                 1
Extras (lb13, w7)                   20
                                    --
Total (9 wkts, 50 overs)           235
```

Fall of wickets: 1–40, 2–55, 3–100, 4–105, 5–143, 6–179, 7–187, 8–215, 9–232.

Bowling: Hughes 8–0–43–2; Reiffel 10–2–42–2; Blewett 8–0–44–1; George 10–1–33–1; McIntyre 10–0–45–3; Martyn 4–0–15–0.

Umpires: D Hair and T A Prue

Australia A beat England by 29 runs

OTHER RESULTS Dec 2: Aust bt Zimb by 2 wkts. **Dec 4:** Aust A bt Zimb by 5 wkts. **Dec 6:** Aust bt Eng by 28 runs. **Dec 8:** Aust bt Zimb by 84 runs. **Dec 10:** Aust A bt Zimb by 7 wkts. **Dec 11:** Aust bt Aust A by 6 runs. **Dec 13:** Eng bt Aust A by 31 runs. **Dec 15:** Zimb bt Eng by 13 runs. **Jan 7:** Eng bt Zimb by 26 runs. **Jan 8:** Aust bt Aust A by 34 runs. **Jan 10:** Eng bt Aust by 37 runs.

Figure 7.24   The cricket score on the *Electronic Telegraph*.

Where are we now?

If we look at the two extensive examples here, it is tempting to view the information hierarchically. For example, the BBC's server reflects the structure of the organization and the underlying commerce. The *Telegraph*'s server clearly

A child gives the Pope a hat

Figure 7.25   Photograph from the *Electronic Telegraph*.

reflects the structure of a printed newspaper. At least, that is the first impression and it is unfortunately reinforced by seeing the examples printed here. However, as soon one accesses the servers live, the richer structure becomes apparent, with cross-links between subjects, pages giving different views onto the same data, thus giving a fresh perspective, and interactive, dynamic information, for example where contributions are added by subscribers.

We hope that, armed with the examples in these chapters, you can now figure out how to build your own information service and use this technology to make it available to your friends, customers and even people whom you will never know.

Chapter 8
Servers galore

In this chapter we shall go into some detail on the configuration of a few of the most popular WWW servers – NCSA's HTTPD, CERN's HTTPD and MacHTTP. As new releases of these servers become available, the information given here will become incomplete, but server writers do attempt to maintain compatibility with previous versions. You should use this chapter as a guide as to the functionality available, but also check the latest online data when installing a server. A list of relevant URLs is given in Appendix E.

Available servers

There are many WWW servers available and more seem to be released each month. We shall list all the known servers, but there is not space here to go into detail on each of them, so we will concentrate on a few of the more popular ones.

At the time of writing CERN's "list of available servers", available with the URL

```
http://info.cern.ch/hypertext/WWW/Daemon/Overview.html
```

lists the following servers. We do not give the individual URLs here, as some of them would quickly become out of date; instead we encourage you to look at CERN's list first.

- CERN HTTPD   The W3 daemon program, full featured, with access authorization, research tools, and so on. This daemon is also used as a basis for many other types of server and gateways. Can also act as a caching proxy server. Authors: Ari Luotonen, Henrik Frystyk, Tim Berners-Lee. *Platforms:* Unix, VMS.

- NCSA HTTPD   The other very widely used WWW server for Unix sys-

tems. It is written in C, and is freely available in the public domain. Many features are similar to CERN's HTTPD. An MS Windows version is also available with most of the features of the Unix version.
Platforms: Unix, MS Windows.

- **GWHIS Server**   Specialized WWW Servers. Commercial, from Quadralay, Inc.
Platform: Unix.

- **Netsite**   Commercially supported server from Netscape Communications Inc.
Platform: Unix.

- **GN**   A single server providing both HTTP and Gopher access to the same data. In C, General Public License. Designed to help the transition of servers from Gopher to WWW.
Platform: Unix.

- **Plexus**   Tony Sander's server originally based on Marc Van Heyningen's Perl Server, but incorporating lots more stuff, including an Archie gateway. It is available in the public domain.
Platform: Unix.

- **MacHTTP**   Server for the Apple Macintosh from Chuck Shotton at the University of Texas at Houston. It is shareware, in that you can retrieve a copy to evaluate, but then must pay to register it.
Platform: Apple Macintosh.

- **SerWeb**   WWW server that runs under Microsoft Windows 3.1. It is fairly simple, and really needs a dedicated machine to run.
Platforms: MS Windows 3.1, MS Windows NT

- **WEB4HAM**   Another windows based server.
Platform: MS Windows.

- **HTTPS for Windows/NT**   Server for Microsoft Windows NT from Chris Adie at the University of Edinburgh. Faster than SerWeb on Windows NT as it is multi-threaded.
Platforms: Windows NT on Intel and Alpha architectures.

- **OS2HTTPD**   An OS/2 server, written by Frankie Fan.
Platform: OS/2.

- **KA9Q NOS**   An Internet server package for DOS that includes HTTP and Gopher Servers.
Platform: DOS.

- **VAX/VMS Server**   Server for systems running DEC VAX/VMS from David Jones at Ohio State University. Uses DEC threads for speed.
Platform: VMS.

- **REXX for VM**   A server consisting of a small C program that passes control to a server written in REXX. C part by Tim Berners-Lee, REXX part by Bernd Pollermann, both at CERN.
  Platform: VM.

- **HTTP for VM**   By R.M. Troth.
  Platform: VM

- **Jungle**   Server in Tk/TCL being written by Lindsay Marshall at the University of Newcastle, UK.
  Platform: Unix.

- **CL-HTTP**   A full-featured, object-oriented HTTP server written in Common Lisp by John Mallery at the MIT Artificial Intelligence Laboratory. Platforms: Symbolics Lisp Machines; ports are underway to Lisps for the Mac and other platforms.

We shall concentrate on NCSA and CERN's HTTPDs for Unix platforms and MacHTTP for Apple Macintoshes.

MacHTTP (version 1.3)

MacHTTP is from Chuck Shotton of the University of Texas at Houston. From version 1.3 onwards it is no longer free, though for private use it is not expensive. There is a 30 day free trial period for evaluation purposes – after that you have to pay. It runs on Quadras, PowerMacs and Mac IIs (we have also tried it on a Powerbook 180 without any problems).

Installation of MacHTTP is extremely simple – it is supplied as a BinHexed Stuffit file. Stuffit is a common archive format on the Macintosh, and BinHex is a common Mac representation that enables binary files to be sent by email without corruption – decoders for both are freely available. Once it has been unstuffed it can simply be run with no additional configuration. For its more elaborate features, it makes use of Apple's AppleScript language, and the AppleScript extensions (which are covered under the licence agreement and supplied with MacHTTP) must be installed.

Configuration

MacHTTP has only one configuration file called `Machttp.config`, which should be tailored to tweak performance, to enable security features and to specify the mappings between Mac file types and MIME content types.

If you simply want to run a server with the more common MIME content types, with no restrictions on who can access your server, then the settings in the default configuration file that comes with the server will get you started.

MacHTTP allows various performance criteria to be set from its configuration file, but their setting requires you to monitor your system to decide their values, and so they are not described here.

Restricting access to a MacHTTP server

If you want to restrict who can access your server you can add a set of restrictions as follows:

```
DENY 128.16.64.
ALLOW 128.16.
```

The default, if you do not specify anything is equivalent to ALLOW *all*. If you do add any restrictions, then the default becomes DENY *all* and you must explicitly enable access from particular sites. Thus the above only allows access from machines with addresses 128.16.something.something, with the exception of machines with address 128.16.64.something.

Specifying the MIME content type with MacHTTP

The configuration file also lets you specify up to 20 MIME content types. A few of the default examples are:

```
TEXT      .HTML      TEXT   *      text/html
BINARY    .GIF       GIFf   *      image/gif
APPL      .EXE       APPL   *      text/html
SCRIPT    .SCRIPT    TEXT   *      text/html
TEXT      .TXT       TEXT   *      text/plain
TEXT      .HQX       TEXT   *      application/mac-binhex40
BINARY    .MOV       MooV   *      video/quicktime
BINARY    .WORD      WDBN   MSWD   application/msword
```

The format here is TYPE, then *File name extension, Mac file type, Creating application*, and finally MIME *content type*. The list is checked for a match in the order: Name extension, Mac file type, Creating application, and the first match determines the MIME content type that the server returns to the client.

Apple Macintoshes normally exclusively use the Mac file type to determine what to do with a data file. However, while this may be sufficient to decide which editor to start to edit a file, it will not distinguish between HTML files, which need a content-type of text/html, and plain text files, needing a content type of text/plain. Also, it would not help much for files that originated on a non-Macintosh system; the Mac file type could be edited using ResEdit, but this would have to be done manually for every file.

119

The first field in these configuration entries is the Machttp.conf command specifying that this is a definition. The different types are needed to decide what to do with the file. BINARY files are simply returned to the client. TEXT files have carriage returns mapped to CR/LF pairs (this is the WWW standard for text files). SCRIPT files are AppleScript files that are fed to AppleScript and executed – they should normally return HTML as output. APPL files are Mac binaries and are simply executed – again they should return HTML as output. See the section on active maps later in this chapter for an example of an AppleScript script with MacHTTP.

NCSA's HTTPD server (version 1.3)

HTTPD from the National Center for Supercomputing Applications (NCSA) in Illinois is one of the most widely used WWW servers on Unix systems. It is public domain and is available for most popular Unix workstations in both source and binary forms.

Configuration

HTTPD has a set of configuration files located in the conf directory. The location of this directory depends on the options you give in HTTPD's makefile when you build it, but the default is /usr/local/etc/httpd. It can also be specified using the ServerRoot command in httpd.conf. For example,

```
httpd -f /usr/local/mydir/httpd.conf
```

specifies where to find httpd.conf, which can then specify where to find the other files.

There are three essential configuration files: srm.conf defines what is located where; httpd.conf defines how HTTPD behaves; and access.conf defines access control restrictions.

The default files supplied with the server all contain comments that make it fairly clear what the directives do. However, we will explain the most important directives in a little more detail.

Setting the server resource map srm.conf

- DocumentRoot /www/htdocs This is the directory that forms the root of the directory tree as seen in URLs. For instance, with DocumentRoot set to /www/htdocs, the URL

  ```
  http://www.host.name/subdir/index.html
  ```

would correspond to the file /www/htdocs/subdir/index.html.

- **UserDir public_html**   HTTPD allows URLs of the form

  http://www.host.name/~a_user/mydir/index.html

  If /usr/home/a_user is the home directory of the user with username a_user, then specifying UserDir to be public_html means that this URL would be expanded to

  /usr/home/a_user/public_html/mydir/index.html

  Of course this directory has to be readable by the user id that the WWW server is being run with. The notation ~a_user is often used to denote the home filestore of the user with username a_user.

- **DirectoryIndex index.html**   When a client requests a URL without specifying a filename within a directory, this is the name of the file HTTPD looks for to return. For instance, with DirectoryIndex set to index.html, the URL http://www.host.name/mydir/ would fetch the file mydir/index.html.

- **AccessFileName .htaccess**   HTTPD allows two ways of specifying access control mechanisms on a per directory basis. One is to have an entry per directory in the access.conf file in the configuration directory. The second is to put an access file in each directory you want to protect. The value specified for AccessFileName says what these per directory access files will be called if they exist.

- **AddType image/jpeg .jpeg .jpg**   AddType lets you add MIME types (see Chapter 5) in addition to the standard ones, or to specify new file extensions for existing MIME types. For example, if we have software that generates filenames with both .jpg and .jpeg extensions, the above entry would specify that both extensions denote a JPEG image file.

- **Redirect /list.html http://www.cs.ucl.ac.uk/index.html** Redirect allows you to tell clients where a document has moved to. For instance, if you used to maintain a list of servers, but no longer have the time to do so, you may redirect people who use your page to someone else's list. Redirection is usually transparent to the user.

- **Alias /local/pubs.html /misc/uk/london/pubs.html**   Specifying Alias values allow you to move files around on your server without breaking any links anyone else may have to them. For instance, if you have a directory called local that is getting cluttered, you could specify the alias above and move the actual file to misc/uk/london/pubs.html. You should avoid overuse of this facility.

- **ScriptAlias /cgi-bin /www/cgi-bin**   Specifying ScriptAlias values allows you to say which directories contain commands to be executed, rather than files to be retrieved. You may specify several different ScriptAlias entries if you wish. Specifying the script alias of /cgi-bin to be /www/cgi-bin as above says that URLs of the form

http://www.host.name/cgi-bin/date

should be dealt with by running the date program that is located in the /www/cgi-bin directory. See the section on CGI in Chapter 5 for details about passing arguments to CGI programs.

srm.conf can also contain a number of other commands, such as those that let you configure automatic indexing of directories.

The server configuration file – httpd.conf

- **ServerType standalone**   ServerType can be either standalone or inetd. On a Unix system, a WWW server can either be started up at system startup or be run from inetd (the Internet daemon, which has a configuration file that specifies that when an incoming connection arrives on a particular port, the corresponding program will be started up to handle that connection). If you run from inetd, the WWW server will only start when a WWW client connects to the server's machine. If you run standalone, a WWW server process should be started up when your machine boots, and will then exist all the time, even when no connections are present. Generally servers that get accessed frequently should be run standalone for performance reasons.

- **Port 80**   This specifies the TCP port for the server to listen on. Port 80 is the default HTTP port, but on a Unix system ports below 1024 are "reserved" and ordinary user programs cannot access them. Thus if you want to run on port 80, the server will have to run as root and then switch to running with the desired user id after startup. If you do not run on port 80, your URLs must include the port number after the machine name.

- **User wwwowner and Group www**   These two directives specify the username and group for a standalone server, started as root, to change to after startup. Leaving the server running as root is extremely inadvisable for security reasons, so if you run your server standalone on port 80, you should set these two parameters.

- **ServerAdmin webweaver@cs.ucl.ac.uk**   ServerAdmin specifies the email address the server will give for people to contact when something goes wrong.

• ServerRoot /var/spool/httpd/ The directory in which the server's configuration, error and log files are kept.

httpd.conf also lets you specify what the error log and access log files are called.

The access configuration file – access.conf

The file access.conf allows you to enable access control on your server. By default, any files in the WWW server's directory subtree are accessible. For instance, a fairly open server with one directory accessible only by people at UCL may have the access.conf file:

```
<Directory /www/htdocs>
<Limit GET>
order allow, deny
allow from all
</Limit>
</Directory>

<Directory /www/htdocs/people/secure>
<Limit GET>
order deny, allow
deny from all
allow from .ucl.ac.uk
</Limit>
</Directory>
```

The file consists of a sequence of <Directory> entries. Each directory entry controls access to the file system subtree rooted at that directory. Each directory entry can also contain access limitations for the different HTTP access methods using the Limit command. The basic form of access control for each method consists of a list of allow and deny entries and, optionally, a set of require entries for password authorization. You can allow or deny individual hosts, domains and even countries. For example, the directory

/www/htdocs/people/secure

in the above is only visible to people whose domain matches .ucl.ac.uk. This would therefore allow speedy.cs.ucl.ac.uk to access the directory, but not rodent.jnt.ac.uk. If two entries (other than the default) match and contradict each other, the order command says which one of the two rules, deny or allow, is applied.

Restricting users

The access.conf file can also be used to provide password authorization to files or directories. Several options are needed for each <Directory> specification to enable this:

- AuthUserFile
- AuthGroupFile
- AuthName
- AuthType

The AuthUserFile option specifies the password file to be used as a list of known users and their passwords. The password file can be maintained using the htpasswd program available with NCSA HTTPD. The AuthGroupFile option specifies a file containing groups of users. Each entry in this file is of the form:

```
webweavers: handley crowcroft
syspeople: jonathan barry rae steve
```

where webweavers is a group name, and handley, crowcroft etc. are usernames as specified in the AuthUserFile.

AuthName specifies a string of text that will be displayed by the client to remind the user which password is required. AuthType is the authorization type, but currently it can only be Basic. These are used along with the require directive as follows:

```
<Directory /www/htdocs/people/secure>
AuthUserFile /www/Admin/passwd
AuthGroupFile /www/Admin/group
AuthName test27
AuthType Basic
<Limit GET>
require group webweavers
require user jonathan
</Limit>
</Directory>
```

More detailed access control

Two other configuration settings can also be specified on a per directory basis: Options and AllowOverride.

```
<Directory /www/htdocs/people/secure>
Options Indexes ExecCGI
AllowOverride Limit AuthConfig
<Limit GET>
</Limit>
allow from all
</Directory>
```

Options can specify None, All, or a combination of Indexes, Includes, IncludesNoExec, FollowSymLinks, SymLinksIfOwnerMatch and ExecCGI. The meanings of these are:

- Indexes specifies that if no default index is available for the directory, the server should list the files in the directory. If the directory contains work in progress or files you do not want the user to see until the appropriate time, either add an index file, or do not specify Indexes.

- Includes specifies that server side include files are enabled in this directory. Server side includes are a method by which the NCSA server parses the HTML document being returned and then includes information from other files, or executes commands to produce data to be included in the document to be returned. Although this is a powerful feature, it can be a security risk in untrusted directories. It is not described in detail here.

- IncludesNoExec allows server side includes, but disables the exec feature. This allows other documents to be included by the server in the document to be returned, but does not allow arbitrary shell or CGI scripts to be run. This somewhat reduces the security risk of server side includes.

- FollowSymLinks specifies that symbolic links in this directory can be followed. If this directory is one in which untrusted users can create files, then specifying FollowSymLinks is a security risk.

- SymLinksIfOwnerMatch specifies that symbolic links in this directory can be followed if the target directory has the same owner as the link.

- ExecCGI specifies that execution of CGI scripts is allowed in this directory.

AllowOverride can be set to None, All, or any combination of Options, FileInfo, AuthConfig, and Limit.

It is advisable to keep access control functionality in one place – namely the access.conf file. However, if you want untrusted users to be able to write their own HTML files, you may also want them to be able to specify access control to their files. Allowing such users access to your access.conf file is extremely inadvisable, so you can let such users set up their own .htaccess files. However, allowing untrusted users to override your security set-up from their own .htaccess file is also inadvisable, as, for instance, they could put in symbolic links to otherwise protected parts of the filestore, which could then be followed by the server. If possible, it is advisable to set Allow-Override to None.

- Options specifies that the .htaccess file can override the Options as specified in access.conf.
- FileInfo specifies that the .htaccess file can use the AddType and AddEncoding directives (as in srm.conf) to add new MIME content types.
- AuthConfig specifies that the .htaccess file can use the AuthName, AuthType, AuthUserFile and AuthGroupFile directives to set user password authorization.
- Limit specifies that the .htaccess file can override who can access the directory.

If no AllowOverride directive is given for a directory or any of its parents, HTTPD assumes AllowOverride All.

Note that the access.conf file applies to a directory subtree, whereas .htaccess files need not override the whole subtree.

Where to configure access control

We said above that it is advisable to keep as much of the access control configuration in one place as possible – namely the access.conf file. However, there are times when this may not be such a good idea.

If you require many different people to configure access control from different files or directories, then using per-directory .htaccess files is preferable. Furthermore, if you have a very long list of access restrictions, using .htaccess files is preferable to avoid having to burden the server with all the access control restrictions for directories that are not relevant.

However, maintaining many .htaccess files is difficult and they often become out of date as your users and their machines change. There is clearly a balance to be struck here, but precisely what combination of the two mechanisms you should use will depend on your usage and your users.

CERN HTTPD (version 3.0)

The CERN HTTPD server is probably the most fully featured WWW server. It supports much the same range of features as NCSA's server, with the addition of acting as a caching proxy server.

Configuration

CERN HTTPD requires a single configuration file to function. By default, CERN HTTPD looks for this file as /etc/httpd.conf, but it can be held elsewhere and the server told where it is using the -r command line flag.

The list of configuration options that CERN HTTPD supports is very extensive and we encourage you to read the document *CERN HTTPD Reference Manual*. Most of the default options are fine to get you started. The ones below are the most important to understand. Note that the order of Pass, Exec, Fail and Map rules is very important.

- ServerRoot /usr/www   This directive specifies the server's home directory. By default the server looks in the icons subdirectory of ServerRoot for its gateway icon files.

- HostName www.rummidge.ac.uk   Set this to the full domain name of your server, for example, www.rummidge.ac.uk. Only necessary if your server does not produce its full domain name in response to redirection requests, but it is not a bad idea to set it anyway.

- Port 80   This specifies the TCP port for the server to listen on. Port 80 is the default http port, but on a Unix system ports below 1024 are "reserved" and ordinary user programs cannot access them. Thus if you want to run on port 80, then the server will have to run as root and switch to running with the desired user id after startup. If you do not run on port 80, your URLs must include the port number after the machine name.

- UserId wwwowner and GroupId www   These two directives specify the username and group for a standalone server started as root to change to after startup. Leaving the server running as root is inadvisable for security reasons, so by default it then changes to run as user nobody with group nogroup. If you run your server standalone on port 80, and you want it to run as a specific user, you should set these two parameters.

- Welcome home.html   The value of Welcome specifies the default file to return when only a directory name is specified in the URL. The defaults are Welcome.html, welcome.html and index.html.

- UserDir public_html   HTTPD allows URLs of the form

  http://www.host.name/~a_user/mydir/index.html

  Setting UserDir to public_html means that this URL would be expanded to /usr/home/a_user/public_html/mydir/index.html
  if /usr/home/a_user is the home directory of the user with username a_user. Of course this directory has to be readable by the user id that the WWW server is being run with.

127

- **Exec /cgi-bin/* /usr/www/cgi-bin/*** Exec specifies that URLs that match the first parameter refer to scripts and are mapped onto a file using the second parameter as a template. For instance, the example above would map a URL such as:

  http://www.host.name/cgi-bin/date

  onto the script file /usr/www/cgi-bin/date, which would then be executed. A more complex example would be the URL:

  http://www.host/cgi-bin/htimage/www/map/uk_map?404,451

  Here the above Exec rule would map the URL onto the script

  /usr/www/cgi-bin/htimage

  and it would pass the additional information /www/map/uk_map and 404,451 into the script in the environment variables PATH_INFO and QUERY_STRING, as defined in the CGI specification. If a URL matches an Exec rule, no further rules will be processed for that request.

- **Pass /* /usr/www/htdocs/*** Pass specifies that if the URL matches the first parameter, it should be mapped onto a file using the second parameter as a template and return the file. For instance, the example given above would map the URL

  http://www.rummidge.ac.uk/index.html

  onto the file /usr/www/htdocs/index.html, which would then be returned to the client. If the URL matches, no further rules from this rules file will be processed for this request, so a general Pass rule such as shown here should be put after any Map or Exec rules or the latter will never be processed.

- **Map /cgi-bin/img/* /cgi-bin/htimage/usr/www/img/*** The Map command provides translation of the filename in the URL. Thus the rule sequence:

  Map /* /usr/www/htdocs/*
  Pass /*

  is functionally equivalent to:

  Pass /* /usr/www/htdocs/*

  The example given above,

  Map /img/* /cgi-bin/htimage/usr/www/img/*
  Exec /cgi-bin/* /usr/www/cgi-bin/*

  would allow the use of the short URL:

```
http://www.host/img/uk_map?404,451
```

in place of the much longer:

```
http://www.host/cgi-bin/htimage/usr/www/img/uk_ map?404,451
```

with exactly the same behaviour. First /img/uk_map?404,451 matches the Map rule and gets translated to

```
/cgi-bin/htimage/usr/www/img/uk_map?404,451
```

which then matches the Exec rule. Note that the order of rules in the rules file is very important here.

- **Redirect /list.html http://www.cs.ucl.ac.uk/index.html** Redirect allows you to tell clients where a document has moved to. For instance if you used to maintain a list of servers, but no longer have the time to do so, you may redirect people who use your page to someone else's list. Redirection is usually transparent to the user. Redirect can also be used to redirect whole subtrees using wildcard (*) matches. Of course a Redirect rule must precede any Pass or Exec rules that would otherwise match the URL.

Enabling security on the CERN server

The CERN HTTPD server has a fairly sophisticated set of security features that can be enabled. Basically, they fall into three categories:

- restricting hosts that can access areas of the server;
- restricting users who can access areas of the server;
- restricting access to individual files.

Restricting hosts

This is most simply done by defining an access class in the server configuration file, and then using the Protect command to restrict access. An example is:

```
Protection UK_ACADEMIC {
    AuthTypeBasic
    GetMask @*.ac.uk, @*.ja.net
}
Protect /research-grants/* UK_ACADEMIC
Protect /grant-awards/* UK_ACADEMIC
```

The Protection command here defines an access class called UK_ACADEMIC. This only has a single restriction – that the connecting client must come from a host whose full hostname ends in .ac.uk (i.e. UK academic) or from .ja.net (i.e. the UK academic network itself). The access class UK_ACADEMIC is used to protect files whose URLs begin with /research-grants/ or /grant-awards/. Note that the asterisk (*) is a wild card that matches anything. Thus if we tried to access

```
/research-grants/1995/jan/index.html
```

from the host

```
rat.cs.ucl.ac.uk
```

then we would pass this protection.

Protect commands *must* be put before the relevant Pass command in the configuration file, as the file is read from top to bottom, and if the Pass command is found first, the file will be returned without checking the protection.

Restricting users

If you want to restrict the users who can access a particular area of the server, you would define a protection class as follows:

```
Protection WEBWEAVERS {
    AuthTypeBasic
    PasswordFile /WWW/Admin/passwd
    GetMask handley, crowcroft
}
Protect /secret/* WEBWEAVERS
```

Here, a password file is specified by the Protection command. The password file can be maintained using the htadmn program available with the CERN server. Unix format password files are also understood.

The entries specified here as the GetMask correspond to entries in the password file, and the user will be prompted for a username and password before being able to access the files specified by the Protect command.

More subtle restrictions can be placed by using a group file. If we had the group file called /WWW/Admin/group as follows:

```
webweavers: handley, crowcroft
syspeople:jonathan, barry, ray, steve
trusted: authors, syspeople, anne
uclcs: @*.cs.ucl.ac.uk, @128.16.*, @193.63.58.*
verysecure: trusted@*.cs.ucl.ac.uk
```

this is then used as:

```
Protection VERYSECURE {
AuthTypeBasic
   PasswordFile /WWW/Admin/passwd
   GroupFile /WWW/Admin/group
   GetMask verysecure
}
Protect /secret/* VERYSECURE
```

This would restrict the access to the secret directory to only trusted people, and then only when they connect from a local machine.

Note that the values you can use for GetMask can be user names, group names, or of the form group@address where address contain wildcards. The group part can be left blank if required, which means anyone can connect from the specified host(s).

Protecting access to individual files using access control lists

It is also possible to have an access control list (ACL) in the directory where the actual data files reside. This can specify access to individual files in the directory, and it also has the advantage that users can set up their own access control to their own files without having to be given permission to change the main server configuration file This can be useful in an environment like a university where you do not necessarily trust your own system's users!

An ACL file must be called .www_acl, and it has the form:

```
index.html : GET : @*.cs.ucl.ac.uk
secret*.html: GET,POST : trusted@*.cs.ucl.ac.uk
*.html : GET : webweavers
```

Beware! If any entry matches, access is given. In the above example, the people in the webweavers group can access the secret*.html files, even if they are not connecting from a ucl machine, because the *.html term matches.

The relevant password and group files are identified from the main server configuration file (possible using Protection and either Protect or DefProt commands).

DefProt is used in the same way as Protect except that by itself it does not actually enable any protection. Instead it identifies which password and group files should be used for .www_acl files in a particular subtree. For example, to specify a default password and group file for the entire server, you would add the following to the main server configuration file:

```
Protection DEFAULT {
   AuthType    Basic
   ServerId    UCL
   PasswordFile /www/config/passwd
   GroupFile   /www/config/group
  }
DefProt /*   DEFAULT
```

If there is no relevant Protect or DefProt command, the .www_acl file will cause an error.

Configuring CERN HTTPD as a caching proxy server

CERN HTTPD 3.0 can be configured to perform as a caching proxy server (see the appropriate section in Chapter 5). This is important, because it can greatly improve external performance for your local users and also greatly reduce international traffic.

Caching can be enabled by commands in the main server configuration file. The following is a typical configuration setup:

```
http_proxy http://www.hensa.ac.uk/
gopher_proxy http://www.hensa.ac.uk/
ftp_proxy http://www.hensa.ac.uk/
no_proxy uk
Pass http:*
Pass gopher:*
Pass ftp:*
Caching ON
NoCaching http://www.cs.ucl.ac.uk/*
CacheRoot /cs/research/mice/boom/scratch1/wwwcache
CacheSize 300 M
CacheLastModifiedFactor 0.2
GcDailyGc 2:00
```

The first few lines here configure the server as a proxy server. In this case we have configured the server to be a proxy server for http, gopher and ftp using the Pass commands. We have also configured it to use an outer proxy server at www.hensa.ac.uk for sites that are not in the UK.

The next few lines configure the way the cache behaves. CacheSize configures the maximum amount of space the server is to use for its cache – in the case 300 MBytes. CacheRoot specifies the directory to store the cache temporary files in. Note that if your system manager backs up your filestore periodically, these cache files should not be backed up or they will add unnecessary load on your backup system.

The last two lines take a little more explanation:

- `CacheLastModifiedFactor 0.2` This specifies how long files are kept for if no expiry date is given by the remote server. If the remote server returns a last modified date that says the file last changed five months ago, then a `CacheLastModifiedFactor` of 0.2 says to keep that file for a further one month (i.e. 0.2×5 months).

- `GcDailyGc 2:00` When the cache size limit is reached, the server will perform garbage collection, that is, it will remove expired files and will then remove other old files that take up too much space until the cache occupies less than the size limit. However, this may mean that old files are kept around long after they are needed. Therefore, if you want to use their disk space for anything else, enabling daily garbage collection maybe a good idea. The `GcDailyGc` command specifies the time of day (using a 24 hour clock) to run the garbage collection.

A number of other cache control commands are also available for use in the server configuration file; these are described in more detail in the *CERN HTTPD Reference Manual*.

Imagemap configuration

There are a number of pieces of software available to help you configure active maps. We will look first at writing your own script, using AppleScript with MacHTTP, to deal with active maps. Then we will look at some of the software designed to make this easier – `imagemap` with NCSA HTTPD and `htimage` with CERN HTTPD. There is now software available for both Macintoshes and PCs that is similar to NCSA's `imagemap` program (they use the same image configuration files) so the DIY (do it yourself) approach is not the only way to implement active maps on the Mac.

Imagemaps using MacHTTP – the DIY approach

MacHTTP's way of implementing imagemaps is to pass the query parameters into a script program written in AppleScript. By default, MacHTTP recognizes any filename ending with `.script` to be an AppleScript program, which it then runs with the correct parameters and which returns the result directly to the remote client.

Unlike NCSA or CERN HTTPDs for Unix systems, MacHTTP does not come bundled with a special `imagemap` program or map definition syntax for defining hotspots in images. Until recently, crafting your own script using

AppleScript was your only option. However, a program called MacImage has recently been released, which is very similar to NCSA's imagemap program described below, and means that the DIY approach is not the only option for MacHTTP users.

Before MacImage, implementation of complex imagemaps using MacHTTP was quite difficult. You had to write your own map script for every active map you wanted to set up. For simple maps, this is not too difficult if you use the example below as a template for your own script. If you haven't met AppleScript before, ignore the first part of the example and just modify the last bit after the comment "--now we're ready to actually do something." Note that like most programming languages, AppleScript is very unforgiving of typing mistakes, so if you have not programmed before, be very careful to ensure you do not miss any characters

The best way to implement active maps is to make use of HTTP's redirection using the found response. This lets the WWW server tell the client where to go to find the actual data it was looking for. The following AppleScript shows one way this can be done (the ⏎ character indicates that there should be no line break).

```
set crlf to (ASCII character 13) & (ASCII character 10)

--this is the header we'll return for active areas of the map
set found_header to "HTTP/1.0 302 FOUND" & crlf & ⏎
    "Server: MacHTTP" & crlf & "MIME-Version: 1.0" & crlf

--this is the header we'll return for errors
set error_header to "HTTP/1.0 400 Bad Request" & crlf & ⏎
    "Server: MacHTTP" & crlf & "MIME-Version: 1.0" & crlf & ⏎
    "Content-Type: text/html" & crlf & crlf

--this is the header we'll return for inactive areas of the map
set unfound_header to "HTTP/1.0 404 OK" & crlf & ⏎
    "Server: MacHTTP" & crlf & "MIME-Version: 1.0" & crlf & ⏎
    "Content-Type: text/html" & crlf & crlf

--parse the arguments to the script
if http_search_args = "" then
    return error_header & "<h1>Bad Request</h1>" & crlf & ⏎
    "Insufficient arguments to image map script"
else
    set comma to offset of "," in http_search_args
    set theLast to count http_search_args
    set x to (text 1 thru (comma - 1) of http_search_args) + 0
    set y to (text (comma + 1) thru theLast of ⏎
http_search_args) + 0
end if
```

```
--now we're ready to actually do something
if x < 16 and y < 16 then
   return found_header & "Location: http://eek/page1.html" & crlf
else if x > 10 and x < 20 and y > 10 and y < 20
   return found_header & "Location: http://eek/page2.html" & crlf
else
   return unfound_header & "<h1>Not found</h1>" & crlf & ↵
   "Nothing found at this map location" & crlf
end if
```

However this is much less elegant than the imagemap mechanism that NCSA's server provides on Unix systems.

NCSA HTTPD's imagemap command

NCSA's HTTPD has a special directory called cgi-bin, in which you can put commands you want to be accessible by the server. (The name cgi-bin is actually configurable as a ScriptAlias from the server's configuration file srm.conf.) One of the pre-supplied commands is imagemap, which is a much more sophisticated active map facility. If we had the following lines of HTML in a document

```
<a href=/cgi-bin/imagemap/uk_map>
<img src=uk_map.gif ISMAP>
</a>
```

then when the user clicked at (say) point (404,451), the client would submit a GET request to the server:

```
GET /cgi-bin/imagemap/uk_map?404,451 HTTP/1.0
```

This calls the imagemap script in cgi-bin with two pieces of information – the QUERY_STRING environment variable with a value of 404,451 and the PATH_TRANSLATED environment variable with a value such as

```
/www/htdocs/uk_map
```

(where /www/htdocs is the root of the server's document tree).

HTTPD has a configuration directory called conf, which contains all the server configuration files. (The location of the configuration directory is set using the ServerRoot command in the httpd.conf file.) Imagemap looks in this directory for a file called imagemap.conf.

In our particular case (we have a few image maps set up), this configuration file looks like:

```
lon_map:/www/conf/london.map
uk_map:/www/conf/uk.map
Worldmap:/www/htdocs/BBC/wrldserv/maps/World_map_image.map
Samerica:/www/htdocs/BBC/wrldserv/maps/Samerica.map
Africa:/www/htdocs/BBC/wrldserv/maps/Africa.map
Central_Asia:/www/htdocs/BBC/wrldserv/maps/Central_Asia.map
Asia:/www/htdocs//BBC/wrldserv/maps/Asia.map
Middle_East:/www/htdocs/BBC/wrldserv/maps/Middle_East.map
Europe:/www/htdocs/BBC/wrldserv/maps/Europe.map
```

Imagemap reads this file, and looks for uk_map, which it finds associated with the file /www/conf/uk.map. It then reads from /www/conf/uk.map, of which the first few entries look like:

```
default http://www.cs.ucl.ac.uk/misc/uk/intro.html#map
#London
circle http://www.cs.ucl.ac.uk/misc/uk/london.html 416 451 396 458
#Canterbury
circle http://www.cs.ucl.ac.uk/misc/uk/canterbury.html 442 463 428 459
#Cambridge
circle http://www.cs.ucl.ac.uk/misc/uk/cambridge.html 413 405 400 407
#Bradford
circle http://www.cs.ucl.ac.uk/misc/uk/bradford.html 337 312 341 311
rect http://www.cs.ucl.ac.uk/misc/uk/bradford.html 335 317 372 325
#Birmingham
rect http://www.cs.ucl.ac.uk/misc/uk/birmingham.html 335 387 394 397
```

Each of these lines describes an active area of the map and the URL associated with that area (lines beginning with a # are comments).

The first entry on a line describes the shape of the active area. The second entry is the URL to redirect the client to if the user clicks within this area. The last arguments give the co-ordinates of the shape. The meaning of the co-ordinates is as follows:

- default *URL*   This gives the URL to go to if the user clicked outside all of the specified shapes.

- rect *URL x1 y1 x2 y2*   This specifies a rectangle with upper left corner $(x1, y1)$ and lower right corner $(x2, y2)$.

- circle *URL x1 y1 x2 y2*   This specifies a circular hot spot with centre $(x1, y1)$ and a point of the edge of the circle $(x2, y2)$.

- poly *URL x1 y1 x2 y2 ... xn yn*   This specifies a hot polygon with vertices $(x1, y1) ... (xn, yn)$. The polygon is automatically closed if the first and last vertices are not the same.

136

Imagemap will run through the file and redirect the client to the URL of the item that best matches (with the exception of default, which only matches if nothing else does).

CERN HTTPD's htimage command

The CERN htimage program is quite similar to the NCSA imagemap program, with the exception that htimage has no master configuration file. If we called htimage from this URL:

```
http://www.host.name/cgi-bin/htimage/usr/www/uk_map?404,451
```

then, assuming the configuration file contains an Exec rule specifying that cgi-bin contains scripts to be executed, htimage would be executed with the QUERY_STRING environment variable set to 404,451 and the PATH_INFO environment variable set to /usr/www/uk_map.

htimage then uses the configuration file /usr/www/uk_map to translate the co-ordinates 404,451. The syntax of the configuration file is similar to NCSA's imagemap. An example file might be:

```
default http://www.cs.ucl.ac.uk/misc/uk/intro.html#map
#London
circle (416,451) 20http://www.cs.ucl.ac.uk/misc/uk/london.html
#Canterbury
circle (442,463) 30http://www.cs.ucl.ac.uk/misc/uk/canterbury.html
#Cambridge
circle (413,405) 35http://www.cs.ucl.ac.uk/misc/uk/cambridge.html
#Bradford
circle (337,312) 18http://www.cs.ucl.ac.uk/misc/uk/bradford.html
rectangle (335,317)(372,325) http://www.cs.ucl.ac.uk/misc/uk/bradford.html
#Birmingham
rectangle (335,387)(394,397) http://www.cs.ucl.ac.uk/misc/uk/birmingham.html
```

There are four allowed keywords in the configuration file:

- default *URL*   This gives the URL to redirect to if the user clicked in none of the specified shapes.
- circle *(x,y) r URL*   This specifies a circle with centre (x, y) and radius r.
- rectangle *(x1,y1) (x2,y2) URL*   This specifies a rectangle with top left corner $(x1, y1)$ and bottom right corner $(x2, y2)$
- polygon *(x1,y1)(x2,y2) . . . (xn,yn) URL*   This specifies a polygon with vertices $(x1, y1) . . . (xn, yn)$. If the first and last points are not the same, htimage will automatically close the polygon.

The abbreviations def, circ, rect and poly are also allowed. The order of the shape definitions in the file is important, as if two shapes overlap, the first one that matches the position clicked on is the one that will be chosen. If the clicked position does not fall within any of the shapes, the default URL will be returned.

Map editors

On Unix systems, the xv program is very useful for creating imagemaps. Simply clicking on the image of the map displayed by xv gives the co-ordinates of

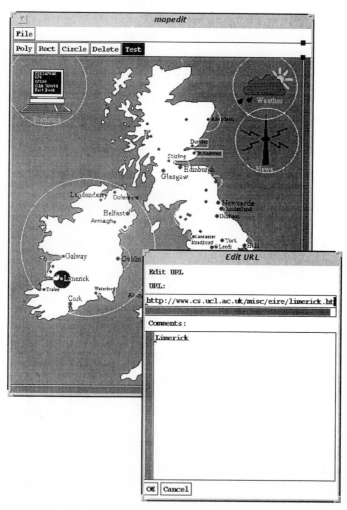

Figure 8.1   Mapedit helps you create imagemap configuration files.

the mouse pointer within the image as required by imagemap. However, there are now a few graphical tools available to help you do this.

A graphical editor called mapedit (see Figure 8.1) has been released for Unix systems, which allows interactive graphical editing of imagemap and htimage configuration files. A similar program called webmap is also available for Apple Macintoshes.

Form processing

Like active maps, handling of forms differs somewhat from server to server. However, as most servers implement the CGI interface, the scripts below should be applicable on many servers. Of course, what the form processing CGI program does to create files and so forth will not necessarily work on different systems.

The DIY approach

The following example is a script written in the Perl language to process the output of our "Pub Feedback" form above. The script should work on servers implementing CGI and the POST method on Unix systems. This does not use any of the available form-parsing programs to make your job easier, so it illustrates what these scripts have to do. (We could have written this in any number of languages, but Perl allows us to illustrate the main points with a relatively short program. Perl is freely available on Unix, DOS, and Macintosh systems.)

```
#!/usr/local/perl
#Read standard input in to "data"
$data = <STDIN>;

#Split the fields up using "$" as the separator
@fields=split(/\&/, $data);

#Go through each field in turn, storing it and URL decoding it
foreach $pair (0..$#fields)
{
    #Split the field into the name of the field (key) and its value
    ($key, $value)=split(/=/, $fields[$pair]);

    #We want to keep the encoded version of this one for later . . .
    if ($key eq "pubname") { $encfilename=$value; }

    #URL decode the field's value . . .
```

```
        #First replace pluses with spaces
        $value =~tr/+/ /;
        #Now split the value into sections with each section starting
        # . . . with an octal code
        @valuebits = split("%", $value);
        foreach $i (1..$#valuebits)
        {
            $thispart=$valuebits[$i];
            #get the two characters comprising the octal code
            $octal=substr($thispart,0,2);
            #convert them to a decimal number
            $decimal=hex("0x".$octal);
            #and replace the octal characters in this part of the string
            #with the ASCII character they should represent
            $valuebits[$i]=pack("C", $decimal).substr($thispart,2);
        }
        #and finally put the sections of the value back together again
        $value=join("", @valuebits);
        #and store it in an associative array for later . . .
        $assocarray{$key}=$value;
}

$filename=$assocarray{"pubname"};
$doc_root="/cs/research/www/www/htdocs";
$fullfilename=$doc_root."/misc/uk/london/pubs/auto"-.$filename.".html";

#Write the entry to a file in HTML
open(OFILE,">".$fullfilename);
print OFILE "<TITLE>", $assocarray{"pubname"}, "</TITLE>\n";
print OFILE "<H1>", $assocarray{"pubname"}, "</H1><HR>\n";
print OFILE "<I>", $assocarray{"pubaddress"}, "</I><P>\n";
print OFILE "<h2>Area:</h2> ", $assocarray{"area"}, "\n";
print OFILE "<h2>Description:</H2>",
    $assocarray{"description"}, "\n";
print OFILE "<h2>Grade: ", $assocarray{"grade"}, "</H2>\n";
print OFILE "1=Average, 2=Worth going to, ",
    "3=Worth a detour, 4=Worth a long detour!\n";
print OFILE "<HR><I>Information submitted by ",
    $assocarray{"username"};
print OFILE " (", $assocarray{"useremail"}, ")\n";
close OFILE;

#Send the entry back to the user so they get some feedback
print "Content-Type: text/html\n\n";
open(INFILE, $longfilename);
```

140

```
print <INFILE>;
close INFILE;

#Add a link to our index file so we can get to the new page
$indexfile=$doc_root."/misc/uk/london/pubs/index.html";
open(IXFILE, ">>".$indexfile);
print IXFILE "<P><a href=\"/misc/uk/london/pubs/auto-"
  .$encfilename.".html\">";
print IXFILE $assocarray{"pubname"}, "</A> ",
  $assocarray{"area"}, "\n";
close IXFILE;
```

The script first reads the form data from its standard input, which is how the server feeds the body of the POST request to a CGI script.

At this stage the form data looks something like:

```
pubname=Northumberland+Arms&pubaddress=Tottenham+Court
+Road%0ANear+Warren+Street+Tube&area=Bloomsbury&descri
ption=UCL+CSs+usual+hangout%21%0A&grade=1&username=Mar
k+Handley&useremail=mhandley@cs.ucl.ac.uk
```

First we separate the data into all the original fields by splitting it at the "&" characters.

Next we separate each field into the field name and the corresponding field value by splitting it at the = character (any equals characters in the data itself will have been coded as octal by the client).

Then we URL decode the value of each field. URL encoding is performed by the browser, replacing spaces with pluses and any special characters with a % followed by the ASCII code of the character in octal. In the server we must reverse this process to obtain the original data.

When we have done all this, we can actually do something with the data – in this case we create a file and write the data to it as HTML, then we send the data back to the user as feedback, and finally we link the new file into our index file so that we can refer to it later.

The cgiparse approach on the CERN server

The CERN HTTPD server comes with a useful script called cgiparse, which does most of the hard work we did above. It will work with either the GET or POST methods, though again we recommend using POST for forms of any length.

cgiparse reads the QUERY_STRING environment variable (as set if you use the GET method) or, if QUERY_STRING is not set, reads CONTENT_LENGTH characters from standard input (as set if you use the POST method). What it does next depends on which flag you give it, but for now we are only interested in the -form flag.

cgiparse -form outputs a string which, when evaluated by the Bourne shell (the standard command interpreter on most Unix systems), sets environment variables (with FORM_ prepended to their names) for each of the form elements. It also URL decodes the variables for you.

Thus a script to do the same task as above (now written in Bourne shell!) would be:

```
#!/bin/sh
eval 'cgiparse -form'
$filename=$FORM_pubname
$doc_root="/cs/research/www/www/htdocs"
$fullfilename=$doc_root"/misc/uk/london/pubs/auto-"$filename".html"

#Write the entry to a file in HTML
echo "<TITLE>"$FORM_pubname"</TITLE>" > $fullfilename
echo "<H1>"$FORM_pubname"</H1><HR>" >> $fullfilename
echo "<I>"$FORM_pubaddress"</I><P>" >> $fullfilename
echo "<h2>Area:</h2> "$FORM_area"\n" >> $fullfilename
echo -n "<h2>Description:</H2>" >> $fullfilename
 . . . and so on . . .
```

cgiparse can take many other command line options to modify its behaviour, and can be used for tasks other than form processing – we recommend the CERN HTTPD *Reference Manual* which is available on the Web for a more detailed explanation.

Using tokenize on MacHTTP

There are as many ways to handle forms with MacHTTP as with all the other servers. In fact, there is a version of Perl for the Mac that can be used with MacHTTP in the same way that AppleScript can be used and, as MacHTTP is CGI compliant, the above Perl scripts should be relatively easily modified for the Macintosh.

If you do not want to install yet another scripting language, AppleScript can also be used to handle forms, though it is made much easier by a few AppleScript extensions. Two extensions, in particular, are recommended – the tokenize extension from Wayne Walrath, which simplifies splitting strings up, and the ScriptTools extensions from Mark Alldrit, which provide enhanced file handling capabilities (amongst other things).

The example below uses tokenize to split the form data into fields at the "&" characters, and then to split the fields into (key, value) pairs at the "=" character. This version does not actually create any files on the server, but how to do so is described in detail in the ScriptTools documentation and examples. This example used the GET method. (The ⏎ character indicates that there should be no line break).

```
set crlf to (ASCII character 13) & (ASCII character 10)
set http_10_header to "HTTP/1.0 200 OK" & crlf & ⏎
   "Server: MacHTTP" & crlf & "MIME-Version: 1.0" & ⏎
   crlf & "Content-type: text/html" & crlf & crlf

--split up the form data at the "&" characters
set form_list to tokenize http_search_args with delimiters "&"

--run through each of the form fields
repeat with i from 1 to count of form_list
   --split each field at the "=" character into a key and a value
   set tmp_list to tokenize (item i of form_list) with delimiters "="
   set tmp_key to first item of tmp_list
   set tmp_value to second item of tmp_list

      --extract the data we want from the fields
      if tmp_key = "pubname"  then
         set title to "<title>" & tmp_value & "<title>" & crlf
         set h1 to "<h1>" & tmp_value & "</h1>" & crlf
      else if tmp_key = "pubaddress" then
         set addr to "<I>" & tmp_value & "</I><P>" & crlf
      else if tmp_key = "description" then
         set desc to "<H2>Description:</H2>" & crlf & "<P>" & ⏎
         tmp_value & "<P>" & crlf
      else if tmp_key = "grade" then
         set grde to "<H2>Grade: " & tmp_value & "</H2>" & crlf
         set expl to "<P>1=Average. 2=Worth going to. " ⏎
         & "3=Worth a detour. 4=Worth a long detour!<P>"
      else if tmp_key = "username" then
         set cred1 to "<hr><I>Information supplied by " & tmp_value & ⏎
         "</i>"
      else if tmp_key = "useremail" then
      set cred2 to " <i>(" & tmp_value & ")</i>"
   end if
end repeat

--and send it back to the user.
return http_10_header & title & h1 & addr & desc & grde & expl & ⏎
cred1 & cred2
```

Server performance

While this chapter should give you enough information to know what the main issues are in setting up and running a WWW server, it is still possible to end up with a server that does not perform too well. If your server is lightly loaded, then this is probably not a problem, so ignore this section. However, if you provide interesting information, your server may be inundated with requests, and you may need to consider its performance. If you are used to systems administration, then the following tips may be obvious, but many servers are run by people with little systems administration experience and, as this group of people is increasing rapidly, we have added a few pointers:

How does your server start?

WWW servers running on Unix (or similar) systems have two ways to start, either from inetd (the Internet daemon) when a connection arrives or at system boot time and the application listens continuously for incoming connections. Starting from inetd is much slower than starting a single copy at system boot time.

Where are the files you are serving actually stored?

Although you may consider your LAN to be fast and your WAN to be slow, if your server has to get your files from a fileserver on a different machine, this will load your LAN unnecessarily and slow down your server's response time. On some systems, it may be possible to use a caching filesystem to do this if you cannot put all the files on the WWW server machine.

How does your server resolve its UID and GID?

Both the CERN and NCSA servers let you start the server as root (so it can use port 80), and then set the user ID and group ID to a non-privileged account. This is a very good idea from a security point of view. However, if your server uses NIS (Network Information System) to obtain the user and group IDs (particularly the supplementary groups), it will have to pull your user and group database files across your LAN from the NIS server for every WWW access. To improve this performance, it may be a good idea to run a slave NIS server on the same machine as the WWW server.

Does your server have enough memory?

It should be fairly obvious, but if a machine is thrashing (the active processes use more memory than is available, so you are continuously paging from disk), then it will perform badly.

On systems such as the Macintosh, there is only one running server, but the memory it uses increases as the number of simultaneous connections increases. Check the server at busy times to ensure its memory allocation is sufficient.

How efficient are your CGI scripts?

If your server is seeing many accesses to CGI scripts, those scripts may dominate the performance of your server. Scripts that do a lot of database searching, or use many files from another fileserver, may cause you problems. If this appears to be a problem, consider running another WWW server on the database machine itself, moving the files to the WWW server or using a caching filesystem to improve the situation.

How stable are your CGI scripts?

It is not uncommon for badly written CGI scripts to contain bugs that cause them to loop indefinitely. While you would probably notice this immediately with a normal program, a WWW user who does not get a response from a server is quite likely to try again – and hit the same bug again.

Some servers can be configured to kill CGI scripts after a certain amount of time. Check how long you think your scripts should take to run and set this value accordingly. However, if you do this, you may never discover malfunctioning scripts unless you set them up write a log entry when they are started and remove the log when they finish correctly.

Have you turned off RFC 931 authentication?

Some servers (such as CERN HTTPD) permit you to enable RFC 931 authentication, which attempts to query the client machine about the username of the person making the request. This information is unreliable at best and, if your server is busy, it is best to disable this feature.

Who are your users?

You can analyze who your users are (or rather where they come from). If many of your users come from one area that is not local to you, consider setting up copies of your data elsewhere.

Have you considered setting up a caching server?

If your server is busy with requests from elsewhere, your local users will get poor performance when accessing the rest of the world. Consider setting up a caching server (such as CERN HTTPD) and configuring your local user's clients to use it. This will help them and will also reduce the load your own users cause elsewhere. If you cannot set up your own caching server (because there is not one available for your hardware), then consider using someone else's. Enquire whether your network provider is running a caching server and, if they are not, then encourage them to do so.

Most of this is common sense if you know a little about how the WWW server actually works. If you have access to any network monitoring facilities, it can be enlightening to look at how much local network access your server is doing when responding to a request. If it is more than you expect, then the server is probably using resources from another local server (such as a fileserver or NIS server) and, if it is excessive, this will be detrimental to performance.

Chapter 9
Problems with WWW

Introduction

The World Wide Web has been a quantum leap for Internet information servers. From the days of typing obscure incantations full of odd names and numbers, we are now able to get at a plethora of different information at the click of a mouse button. However, there are a number of limitations in the World Wide Web at the moment, some due to the underlying network, some due to the implementations of clients and servers and some due to the design of the Web. This chapter is about some of the problems we perceive.

Real time

One key problem with the WWW model is how one can add real time media. Currently, the access protocol model is based on the libWWW RPC approach, where a retrieval is initiated by the request, and the client cannot start displaying the result until the return.

Clearly, if the returned data is very large, then this may be inappropriate (see below). But if the returned data can actually be played as it arrives (e.g. it is audio or video or similar data) then this is clearly not the right way to do things. Two approaches suggest themselves:
- Allow a returned stream of data to be played as it arrives (Netscape does this to a certain extent, but not really for real time applications.).
- Use a separate channel to return real time data

The latter approach is particularly inviting when one considers some of the ways Internet access may be provided in conjunction with cable TV: it is quite possible to deliver broadcast quality TV down current copper twisted pair phone wire, up to modest distances, so long as one uses nearly all the bandwidth in one direction. So one could use a low-bandwidth channel for HTTP access, separate from the high-quality one used for TV. One can envisage other networks where bandwidth is asymmetric, or else there are other technical reasons to separate out channels for delivery of data requests and responses from real-time delivery (or transmission).

TCP + RPC is not a sensible fetch protocol

In the Internet, much useful information is retrieved from a long way away – that is part of its attraction (it is expensive to get using an alternative material approach). However, this means that TCP connections between clients and servers traverse long haul networks. TCP is cleverly designed to avoid congestion (network overload). It has a built in conservatism: in the face of packet loss, it assumes that there are other (existing or new) users sharing the network. It therefore backs off, reducing its sending rate radically (in fact to the minimum effective sending rate conceivable, which is one packet per round-trip time). It then increases this sending rate until around it reaches about half the previous rate that had no loss. It then very slowly increases its sending rate until it finds what is called a "stable operating point", where a single increase may cause a small problem, but not enough to warrant backing right down again. This approach is called *congestion avoidance and slow- start*, and is known as the "linear-increase, exponential-decrease" approach to traffic control. It was devised by Van Jacobson in the late 1980s in response to real network problems.

Now, in the absence of any other knowledge, a new TCP connection must start as it means to go on: slowly. This means that in retrieving a page with a large number of separate calls, a number of "slow-starts" operate, even when there are no other network users and there is no apparent reason to operate these. This causes very jerky response to the client program. Unfortunately, this protocol usage is built right through the stack of protocols between the client, the libWWW and the use of TCP, right through to the semantics of server access.

One way forward would be not to close the connection between the client and server between one HTTP request and the next. Since the server end closes the connection (because of the stateless model described in Chapter 3), this would entail some extra protocol (at least a marker in the stream from the server to the client to inform it of "End of Response"). The server should then operate a timeout to prevent clients that die tying up connection resources in the TCP/IP protocol data space.

In fact, a recent modification to TCP (RFC 1644) specifies an extension that means that TCP can use fewer packets for short exchanges of messages (as RPC and libWWW and HTTP tend to), and can cache information concerning the network performance between one connection and a subsequent one to the same destination. This may well solve a lot of these problems when widely deployed.

Replicas, caches and consistency

Another problem in the World Wide Web is also a result of its good design and a cause of its success: each piece of information is held at the server run by the information provider and is not usually to be found anywhere else. This means that all accesses from no matter which client, no matter where, arrive at the same server. This means that popular servers are hot spots in the network and cause a lot of network traffic, as well as being potentially overloaded by requests in terms of processing power. Since the information users and providers in the Internet are quite often totally disjoint from the network providers, there is no particular match between the resources each provides, and popular servers may be set up much faster than even the most assiduous network providers can re-dimension their communications links.

There are two main solutions for information providers, and third, more political, one involving the network providers:

- **Provide caches**   This is already being done, as was described in Chapter 5. Smart servers can act as clients to other servers. Instead of client programs accessing each and every server around the world, clients always (or usually) access their nearest managed WWW server. It then follows links on their behalf and keeps copies of the data retrieved for future access by the same or other clients. Such caches must be capable of being invalidated (or out-dated) in some way, if the originator of the information decides to withdraw it. This requires servers to keep track of accesses by other servers that are known to cache things, or else some "honesty" mechanism on the part of caching servers, to check whether their cached copy needs updating. (Remember that it will take a lot less time to check the date on an original piece of data than to retrieve it all again, so this could indeed be done every time. HTTP does allow such requests, but these methods are not yet widely developed.) Measurements in 1994 suggest that a single level of caching applied consistently throughout the Internet could reduce traffic by as much as 70 per cent, and increase response times for WWW access and everything else appreciably.

- **Replicas**   Rather than provide "on demand" caches, this approach entails manually tagging data that is likely to be popular and having it replicated across multiple servers when it is installed. Provided that a sensible naming system is in place (URNs, universal resource names, indicating what something is, rather than being tied to where it is, as URLs,

149

addresses, etc., are) clients will again go to an appropriately near server, rather than to the originator all the time. This is already in use in the world wide archive servers and has been very effective in reducing network load for FTP traffic. It is, however, more manual than the previous approach.

- **Migration**   If the network providers were prepared to monitor and release statistics of network access patterns to WWW servers and allow the WWW servers access to topological (link map and bandwidth) information about the network, then it would be possible to migrate information around the network as the *centre* of access patterns from clients became obvious. Again, the naming system must make this feasible transparently to the users.

All three of these mechanisms require the Name/Identity/Address mappings to be in place if they are to work in a completely transparent way and they require an increased degree of intelligence about managing information in the WWW. However, none require centralized management of the Internet or the WWW, so all are still largely in the spirit of the existing successful system.

Two interesting facets of replicas and caches to muse upon are charging for resources, and security. If we cache for someone, we are saving them disk resources. If we do not provide the same assurances about secure access, we are possibly causing them loss of revenue. Both these problems are complex to solve, although as we have seen in Chapter 5, the hooks are there to help provide solutions for all of the problems we have described here, albeit with some extra knowledge on the part of the information managers.

Billing

We discuss charging for the network in the next chapter. Charging for information is, however, a very different matter and will be essential for a number of information providers to offer quality services on the Internet.

The prime requirement is for various degrees of security and we discuss those in the next section. Currently, we would advise against transmitting billing information or credit card information on the Internet unless you have made yourself very familiar with some of this technology.

WWW makes it quite straightforward to account for access and therefore to work out a charging scheme. The user is identifiable (subject to security) and each item retrieved is identifiable, while most servers already provide extensive logging. It is then simply a matter of working out a policy, and implementing it. Note that without a guaranteed service delivery channel (see next chapter) it is hard to bill for timeliness of delivery of information.

Security

Security concerns are typically broken down into the following areas:

- **Privacy**   Under this heading we are talking about non-disclosure of information except to those authorized (typically creator and anyone they wish to transmit it to, subject to proof of identity). If I send something over a communications channel, it is liable to be eavesdropped upon, copied or intercepted in many different ways. The solution is to mangle (encrypt) what is sent so that someone who takes a copy cannot recognize it. The easy way to do this is to have "one-time- codebooks" (e.g. each letter is sent as a number that is its next occurrence in some pre-agreed book). This is inefficient, complex and error prone, and therefore not a lot of use for WWW servers. A more useful technology is cryptography and, in particular, a mechanism called public-key cryptography, of which more below. A less useful (but still effective) technique is private-key cryptography, (such as the US National Security Agency standard DES – Data Encryption Standard).

   All cryptographic technology for privacy is export controlled from the USA at the moment, which means that use every day in the Internet relies on externally produced implementations. Also, for international companies trading in the USA, this is a political obstacle to using such technology for fear of offending the US government.

   In fact, for many WWW servers, privacy may not really be an issue, especially if the function of the server is effectively to add value to other services (advertise). Even if this is not the case, it may simply be to difficult for someone to monitor all WWW traffic from a particular server and piece together all the data from there – but do not count on this one bit.

- **Authentication**   This is to do with proving one's identity and it is a very subtle business. Typically, it relies on some notion of trust. If I transmit something to someone by talking to them face to face, I am assured by their face, or voice, that they are who they say they are. However, I also need to understand their role – do they really work for whom they say they do? Typically, they produce credentials (an expensive-to-fake ID card, for example).

   If I send something over a communications channel, I must also exchange some form of credentials to be assured the receiver is who they say they are (like listening to their voice or looking at their face, I may need a notarized signature etc., etc.). There are a number of techniques for digital signatures that are hard to forge. Luckily, this technology is not subject to US export controls. Systems such as Kerberos and PGP (Pretty Good Privacy) provide authentication, as well as possibly non-exportable privacy.

   Once you have authentication, then a server can be protected from

151

dangerous access. It can then match authenticated credentials to access control lists, and even carry out billing based on these (though it is still better not accept credit card numbers or send bills over the same network until it also has privacy technology).

- **Integrity**   This is to do with making sure that information is not tampered with in transit. It is usually achieved by signing the data with some function (checksum) of the data itself, wrapped up with some secret key that is not transmitted (perhaps has been exchanged previously through public-key cryptography).

- **Non-repudiation of transmission and reception**   Non-repudiation is the facility of a secure system to permit proofs that a sender or receiver were indeed the sender and receiver, i.e. whether you disclose who the sender or receiver is.

We might add another: legal recognition. If you want to charge people for information, exchange contracts over networks, etc., all the security in the world is not much use if it is not backed up by some sort of legal position.

Very, very paranoid sites are concerned with two more security facets: traffic pattern analysis and covert signalling. Traffic pattern analysis might concern finance houses who would be worried if it was known which information providers they were gathering information from in combination, for example, since it might permit others to trade on this knowledge (impending mergers, etc.). Covert signalling is a way of carrying information piggy-backed on legitimate information. This is very handy for spies getting information out of secure sites.

Berners-Lee lists the following specific checklist for existing WWW servers:

- authentication of requests and servers;
- privacy of request and response;
- abuse of server features;
- abuse of servers by exploiting server bugs;
- unwitting effects on the net;
- abuse of logs.

Finally, note that keeping logs is a very important part of security. A secure system will attract more attempts to hack, simply because it poses more of a challenge, but also because there is potentially more monetary gain from hacking a system that someone has apparently spent money to protect. A system always has vulnerabilities (there is no such thing as 100 per cent security, just 100 per cent lack of detected hacks). If you keep audit trails, then it is possible to track a lot more problems. It may also be possible to track the cause of the loophole and fix it.

Finally, always keep backups of valuable data.

Public-key cryptography and the WWW

Public-key cryptography is a very neat technology. Private-key systems involve people sharing a single private key and each person having to give each trusted person a copy of their private key via some secure channel. However, if they have this secure channel, why not just use it anyhow for all communications (actually it may be a more costly channel, but never mind . . .).

The idea of public-key cryptography is that instead of one key, there are two, a private key and a public key. When I create a key, using some fancy maths, I actually create these two interrelated keys. If I encrypt things with my private key, it is decryptable with my public key but not with my private key . . . and vice versa. How is this useful?

Well, I now no longer have the key distribution problem that I had for private keys (needing some magic special secure channel), since I can publish my public key (e.g. in the WWW on my home page).

The popular mail authentication and security package PGP uses such technology, and promises to be directly applicable to WWW.

Chapter 10
Where is WWW heading?

The World Wide Web may, like the Internet, become a victim of its own success.

Multimedia: video and audio support?

Early experiments during the 1970s and 1980s in voice across the Internet never came to full fruition simply as a result of lack of bandwidth. Multimedia file and mail transfer did come about, however, and the MIME content types permit easy use in WWW. Recently, however, researchers have been much more successfully running audio and video interactively across the world because of increases in bandwidth. This has led to the development of interesting tools for computer supported collaborative work (and play). There have been some early attempts to integrate these in WWW, albeit only with partial success. There are three main areas one can look at:

- using WWW Clients to browse indices of existing multimedia databases and transmissions (e.g. TV/radio/video on demand)
- sharing views on the Web by linking up and synchronizing distributed WWW clients (shared Mosaic)
- using WWW as a way to rendezvous, co-ordinate and launch conferencing and other applications (Mbone) (see Figure 10.1).

Spiders and robots

The World Wide Web is very good for browsing. However, owing to its very web-like nature, it is hard to index and therefore hard to search. It is true that many Web server sites have searchable data, but that is done in a local way.

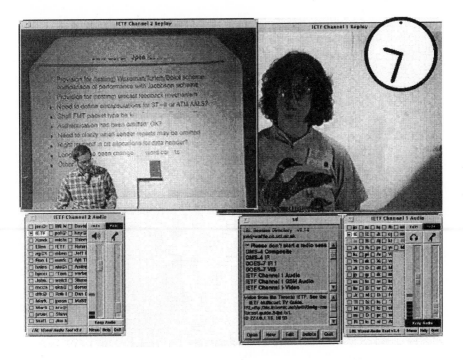

Figure 10.1   Video conferencing on the Internet.

Often, a CGI backend, such as Waisgate, is used (as mentioned earlier) or even some completely local script or database query system.

What is needed is an *inter-site* indexing and searching mechanism as well as these site- and subject-specific *intra-site* schemes. The problem is that the Web grows successfully *because* it permits heterogeneity – each site can choose how to structure its information (and links).

One solution is to provide clients that allow the user to specify searches and then launch these searches on the network. The problem here is that the search will cause a lot of (possibly unnecessary) accesses and load up caches all around the WWW; and this will take a long time. This is, possibly in all respects, anti-social.

The solution is to provide intelligent tools that automatically build indexes of the web, continuously and incrementally as it grows. These are known as spiders or robots or wanderers. There are a variety of them, varying in complexity, but the key idea is simple: starting from a known site or list of sites, simply follow all the links, building a map of all URLs (and titles, and possibly even pulling pages and creating contents indexes through database techniques such as Key-word-in-context). Subsequently, this index can be stored, and possibly even replicated across other sites (or simply rely on caching at other servers when remote clients repeatedly access an index).

To prevent network and server overload, there are a number of rules (of etiquette) to which such spiders are subject. The main requirement is that they judge the frequency with which they visit sites to be low enough not to exceed a typical user threshold, but high enough to keep the index reasonably up to date.

Future enhancements to spiders may include ways to partition the problem across the network, so that load can be localized, and ways to pre-load caches to speed up the index accesses.

There are many different tools, and more are being added monthly, but some of the most popular are

- JumpStation, run by Jonathon Fletcher at Solomon University
- World Wide Web Worm, maintained by Oliver McBryan, at Colorado
- CUI index
- Yahoo
- Lycos
- Mother of all bboards

To exclude a robot or spider from a server, it has been proposed that servers should keep a top-level file, accessible by HTTP and called /robots.txt, which lists the robot type and areas that it cannot access on this server.

Sites that maintain spiders and robots should make sure that the program logs and time stamps its actions, so that problems can be diagnosed and development of these useful facilities is not endangered by being accused (unjustifiably) of overload.

Virtual reality, games and MUDs in general

There are a number of multiplayer interactive Internet games, such as Xtrek. But more interestingly there have emerged in recent years a set of role playing environments known as MUDs (MultiUser Dungeons) or MOOs (after Lambda Moo, one of the original ones).

Some of these (such as the Jupiter project at Xerox PARC) have been extended to include virtual reality (graphical subjective views of rooms and other simulated pieces of the real world).

An exciting development has been the use of the World Wide Web to provide access and structure to such environments, as for example, with Web World. At the time of writing, these have not reached full potential, but they may represent a large market in the future.

156

Problems with the Internet

The growth in CPU memory and storage performance/price has made all these new applications possible. The reduction in connectivity costs is leading to the use of these new applications. The corresponding increase in network functionality has yet to happen. The Internet is experiencing a number of problems because of the growth in its size and in the breadth of the community using it. These include:

- **Scale**   The number of systems is exceeding the available numbers for addressing systems in the Internet – a similar problem that everyone in the UK is accustomed to from time to time with telephone numbers. The way these numbers are allocated is also leading to problems with the amount of memory in the router boxes that hold together the Internet. Currently, these need to hold the full list of every site in the Internet. A more hierarchical approach (like the telephone system or the postal system) will fix this.

- **Security**   Security is really not a question that is relevant when talking about the Internet itself. What needs to be secured are hosts, and information. However, the network must provide relevant hooks for security to be implemented.

- **Billing**   Currently, the charging model in most of the Internet is a leasing one. Bills are for the speed of access, not the amount of usage. However, many believe that at least during busy periods, or else for priority service, billing will be necessary as a negative feedback mechanism. This will also require security so that the right people can be billed legally.

  There are some who believe that every type of Internet access should be billed for on a usage basis. This is problematic and, in fact, it has been shown that it does not maximize profit. Only the user herself knows how "urgent" a file transfer is. With very many types of data around, the net can only charge for the ones it really knows about, such as, say, long-distance voice or high-quality video.

- **Guarantees**   The Internet has not historically provided guarantees of service. Many providers have done so, but typically by over-provisioning the internal resources of their networks. In the long run, this may prove viable, but, at least for the next few years, we will need mechanisms to control guarantees, especially of timeliness of delivery of information. For example many information providers such as the Share Trading and News businesses value their commodity by time.

Performance parameters

There are three key parameters to worry about in the network, and these are important if you intend using a part of the Internet to deliver commercial or dependable WWW services:

- **Errors** Transmission technology is *never* perfect. Even glass fibre has occasional errors. These are when what is received is not what was sent. (Imagine you send a letter by airmail, and the plane crashes at sea, and the postbags are recovered but water damaged – it happens!).

- **Delay or latency** A network is not infinitely fast. In fact, now that we are building a global society, the-speed-of-light limit that Einstein was so keen on, is rearing its pretty head. Furthermore, busy networks run more slowly. Picture the difference between a space shuttle and a canal boat. A canal boat runs at four miles an hour, while the shuttle runs at around seven miles a second. So the time to get there and back is much less on the shuttle. However, there is a limit.

- **Throughput** Different networks are built for different amounts of traffic. The canal system referred to above can carry around 200 tonnes per boat, while the shuttle can only carry around 1 tonne. So while you may have lower latency on some networks, you may also have lower throughput. Normally, though, latency and throughput are largely unconnected.

  Typically, throughput is a feature of how much you pay, while latency is a feature of the distance over which you are communicating, plus the busy-ness of the net.

Internet service model futures

The Internet provides a best-effort service. When you want to send "something", you just send it. You do not have to know that there is a receiver ready, that the path exists between you and a potential receiver or that there are adequate resources along the path for your data. You do not have to give a credit card number or order number so you can be billed. You do not have to check the wire to make sure there are no eavesdroppers.

Some people are uncomfortable with this model. They point out that this makes it hard to carry traffic that needs certain kinds of performance guarantees, to make communication secure or to bill people. These three aspects of the Internet are intimately connected, and in the following sections we examine how research at UCL and elsewhere is leading to a new Internet model which accommodates them.

Best effort and charging

The current model for charging for traffic in the Internet is that sites connect via some "point of presence" of a provider and pay a flat fee per month according to the speed of the line they attach with, whether they use it to capacity or not.

For existing applications traffic and capacity, this model is perfect. Most sites wish to exchange data, which has value that is not increased radically by being delivered immediately. For instance, when I send electronic mail, or transfer a file, the utility to me is in the exchange.

The network providers maximize their profit by admitting all traffic and simply providing a fair share. As the speed decreases, my utility decreases, so I am prepared to pay less. But the increase in possible income from the additional users outweighs this. The underlying constant cost of adding an additional user to the Internet is so low, that this is always true.

However, there are other kinds of traffic that this "best effort" model does not suit at all, and we look at those next.

Real-time traffic

The Internet has now been used for more than four years to carry audio and video traffic around the world. The problem with this traffic is that it requires guarantees: it has a minimum bandwidth below which audio becomes incompressible and even compressed video is unusable. For human interaction, there is also a maximum delay, beyond which conversation becomes intolerable.

In the experimental parts of the Internet, we have re-programmed the routers that provide the interconnection to recognize these kinds of traffic and to give it regular service.

There are two aspects to this: first we must meet the minimum traffic guarantee, and this is done by looking more frequently at the queues of traffic in the net for traffic that needs more capacity. This then also means that the delay seen by this traffic is only affected by the amount of other traffic on the network and the basic transmission time (speed of light, or thereabouts, although around the world, this is still a significant factor – however, it is one we are not at liberty to alter!). As we increase the other traffic, our video or audio data experiences increasing delays and variations of delay. So long as this stays within tolerable limits, the receiver can adapt continuously (e.g. in silences in audio or between video frames) and all is well. Meanwhile, any spare capacity carries the old best effort traffic as before. However, when the total amount of traffic is higher than capacity, things start to break down.

At this point there are three views on how to proceed:

• Engineer the network so that there is enough capacity. This is feasible only while most people's access speed is limited by the "subscriber loop", or tail circuits that go to their homes/offices. When we all have fibre to the home/desk-top, the potential for drowning the net is alarming. Note though, that the telephone network is currently over-engineered, so for audio capacity we could certainly switch everyone over to the Internet, switch all our phones over to Internet-based terminals and have a flat fee model.

- Police the traffic, by asking people who have real-time requirements to make a "call set-up" as they do with the telephone networks. When the net is full, calls are refused, unless someone is prepared to pay a premium and incur the wrath of other users by causing them to be cut off!

- Simply bill people more as the net gets busier. This model is proposed by economists at Harvard, and is similar to models of charging for Road Traffic proposed by the Transport Studies group at UCL. We believe it is optimal. Since we have already reprogrammed the routers to recognize real-time traffic, we have the ability to charge on the basis of logging of this traffic.

Note that we can charge differentially, as well. Previously, until we could make the guarantees, we would have a hard time placing a contract for this. Now it is feasible, but we have maintained all the original advantages of the Internet (no call set-up, easy to rendezvous and so on).

Receiver-driven resource reservation

The addition of multicast, multiple-destination delivery of data to the Internet has led to another refinement of the model: receivers, rather than senders, decide which, and how much, data they need.

In the radio and TV business, this has been the practice for some time. In computer networks, where we wish to find information, it has been less obvious. However, if we are disseminating information unsolicited, then the easiest way to cope with very large scale groups is to copy the TV model and allow people simply to "tune in".

This does not mean that we cannot charge, or that we have no security. These two aspects of the Internet are solved easily. The receivers are the people who specify which groups they join and this information propagates through the routers, which are already supporting audio/video and data distribution at various quality levels. As they log the data, they simply add tags to say which users are currently receiving which information and when. This also allows users who have less good equipment to specify a lower grade delivery and the network can then save resources by only delivering a subset of the data (e.g. lower-resolution video, or lower frame rate). As for security, we simply encrypt all data at source and only users with the correct key can decrypt the data they ask for. This relies on a more open attitude to privacy in networks than has been politically feasible for some time. However, if business is to take real advantage of the Information Superhighway, then it is a requirement, no matter which actual technology is used to deliver the data.

Appendix A

HTML grammar

In these appendices, we have reproduced, to the best of our ability, the grammar for HTML, the specification of URLs, the protocol specification for HTTP, and some relevant pieces of the MIME specification. As usual, the secretary will disavow any knowledge if you find errors or inconsistencies between these versions and the living, true standards documents, obtainable through your RFC or IETF draft server.

These specifications are written in a rather formal language, so first we introduce the idea of *grammar*, as used by networking and computing people.

Introduction to grammars

Grammars are something we may have learned at school. However, those grammars are for *natural* languages, like Chinese, Spanish or English. We remember rules like *subject*, *verb*, *object* and how to conjugate a verb or decline a noun (using cases like nominative, vocative, accusative, therapeutic, etc.).

Computer languages, and we can include communications protocols, are specified using similar meta-rules. Computer languages are a bit simpler, and most are specified using a Grammar of grammars, invented by two great computer scientists, Backus and Naur, and named after them *Backus Naur Form* or BNF.

A BNF consists of a set of *production rules* for sentences in the language. A finished sentence (think of it as a program statement, or in the case of HTML, a document) consists of a collection of *terminals* or base words from the language, put together according to the production rules. The words may be drawn from a simpler grammar called a *lexicon*, which is basically your spelling rules, and they are made up from characters (letters) drawn from an *alphabet*. In any computer grammar, we define all three of these, in tiny, exhaustive (tedious) detail. Alphabets are just lists of letters allowed and lexicons are fairly obvious too, but grammars are less so.

Production rules build up a tree of rules to generate legal sentences. An example of a BNF grammar for a simple language might be:

```
     Alphabet =  'a', 'b', 'c', . . . 'z', '.'
      Lexicon =  amuses, dangerousthings, empowers, fire, holds, puzzles,
                 women
    Utterance =  Subject Verb Object .
      Subject =  Noun
       Object =  Noun
         Noun =  fire | women | dangerousthings
         Verb =  amuse | empower | hold | puzzle
```

So legal utterances in this language would include:

```
    fire holds dangerousthings
    women puzzles fire
    dangerousthings amuses women
    . . .
```

We can see that a compact grammar can describe a huge vista of utterances! The example grammar here is a take-off from a famous real language that was studied extensively by anthropologists and linguists in which a single word was actually used to convey "fire", "women" and "dangerous things". In that language, context was necessary to determine which meaning was intended, whereas in our simple language here the form of the sentence is sufficient.

HTML and SGML

This is a grammar (BNF) for SGML/HTML and is a definition of HTML with respect to SGML. It assumes an understanding of SGML terms.

```
<!DOCTYPE HTML [
<!-- Jul 1 93 -->
<!-- Regarding clause 6.1, SGML Document:

    [1] SGML document = SGML document entity,
        (SGML subdocument entity |
        SGML text entity | non-SGML data entity)*

    The role of SGML document entity is filled by this DTD,
    followed by the conventional HTML data stream.
-->
```

```
<!-- DTD definitions -->

<!ENTITY % heading "H1|H2|H3|H4|H5|H6" >
<!ENTITY % list " UL | OL | DIR | MENU ">
<!ENTITY % literal " XMP | LISTING ">

<!ENTITY % headelement
      " TITLE | NEXTID |ISINDEX" >

<!ENTITY % bodyelement
      "P | HR | %heading |
      %list | DL | ADDRESS | PRE | BLOCKQUOTE
      | %literal">

<!ENTITY % oldstyle "%headelement | %bodyelement | #PCDATA">

<!ENTITY % URL "CDATA"
      --  The term URL means a CDATA attribute
          whose value is a Uniform Resource Locator,
          as defined. (A URN may also be usable here when defined.)
      -->

<!ENTITY % linkattributes
      "NAME NMTOKEN #IMPLIED
      HREF %URL; #IMPLIED
      REL CDATA #IMPLIED -- forward relationship type --
      REV CDATA #IMPLIED -- reversed relationship type
                            to referent data:
                            PARENT CHILD, SIBLING, NEXT, TOP,
                            DEFINITION, UPDATE, ORIGINAL etc. --
      URN CDATA #IMPLIED -- universal resource number --

      TITLE CDATA #IMPLIED -- advisory only --

      METHODS NAMES #IMPLIED -- supported public methods of the object:
                            TEXTSEARCH, GET, HEAD, . . . . --
      ">

<!-- Document Element -->

<!ELEMENT HTML O O (( HEAD | BODY | %oldstyle )*, PLAINTEXT?)>
<!ELEMENT HEAD - - ( TITLE? & ISINDEX? & NEXTID? & LINK* & BASE?)>

<!ELEMENT TITLE - - RCDATA
      -- The TITLE element is not considered part of the flow of text. It
         should be displayed, for example as the page header or window
         title.
      -->
```

```
<!ELEMENT ISINDEX - O EMPTY
        -- WWW clients should offer the option to perform a search on
           documents containing ISINDEX.
        -->

<!ELEMENT NEXTID - O EMPTY>
<!ATTLIST NEXTID N NAME #REQUIRED
        -- The number should be a name suitable for use
           for the ID of a new element. When used, the value
           has its numeric part incremented. EG Z67 becomes Z68
        -->

<!ELEMENT LINK - O EMPTY>
<!ATTLIST LINK
     %linkattributes>

<!ELEMENT BASE - O EMPTY -- Reference context for URLS -->
<!ATTLIST BASE

      HREF %URL; #IMPLIED

   >

<!ENTITY % inline "EM | TT | STRONG | B | I | U |
           CODE | SAMP | KBD | KEY | VAR | DFN | CITE "
     >

<!ELEMENT (%inline;) - - (#PCDATA)>

<!ENTITY % text "#PCDATA | IMG | %inline;">

<!ENTITY % htext "A | %text" - Plus links, no structure ->

<!ENTITY % stext    -- as htext but also nested structure--
           "P | HR | %list | DL | ADDRESS
            | PRE | BLOCKQUOTE
            | %literal | %htext">

<!ELEMENT BODY - - (%bodyelement|%htext;)*>

<!ELEMENT A   - - (%text)>

<!ATTLIST A
     %linkattributes;
     >

<!ELEMENT IMG  - O EMPTY -- Embedded image -->

<!ATTLIST IMG
     SRC %URL; #IMPLIED   -- URL of document to embed --
     >
```

```
<!ELEMENT P   - O EMPTY -- separates paragraphs -->
<!ELEMENT HR  - O EMPTY -- horizontal rule -->

<!ELEMENT ( %heading ) - - (%htext;)+>

<!ELEMENT DL  - - (DT | DD | %stext;)*>

<!--                Content should match
                    ((DT,(%htext;)+)+,(DD,(%stext;)+))
                    But mixed content is messy. -Dan Connolly
   -->

<!ELEMENT DT  - O EMPTY>
<!ELEMENT DD  - O EMPTY>

<!ELEMENT (UL|OL) - - (%htext;|LI|P)+>
<!ELEMENT (DIR|MENU) - - (%htext;|LI)+>
<!--    Content should match ((LI,(%htext;)+)+)
        But mixed content is messy.
  -->
<!ATTLIST (%list)
    COMPACT NAME #IMPLIED -- COMPACT, etc.--
    >

<!ELEMENT LI  - O EMPTY>

<!ELEMENT BLOCKQUOTE - - (%htext;|P)+
    -- for quoting some other source -->

<!ELEMENT ADDRESS - - (%htext;|P)+>

<!ELEMENT PRE - - (#PCDATA|%inline|A|P)+>
<!ATTLIST PRE
    WIDTH NUMBER #implied
    >

<!-- Mnemonic character entities. -->
<!ENTITY AElig  "&#198;" -- capital AE diphthong (ligature) -->
<!ENTITY Aacute "&#193;" -- capital A, acute accent -->
<!ENTITY Acirc  "&#194;" -- capital A, circumflex accent -->
<!ENTITY Agrave "&#192;" -- capital A, grave accent -->
<!ENTITY Aring  "&#197;" -- capital A, ring -->
<!ENTITY Atilde "&#195;" -- capital A, tilde -->
<!ENTITY Auml   "&#196;" -- capital A, dieresis or umlaut mark-->
<!ENTITY Ccedil "&#199;" -- capital C, cedilla -->
<!ENTITY ETH    "&#208;" -- capital Eth, Icelandic -->
<!ENTITY Eacute "&#201;" -- capital E, acute accent -->
<!ENTITY Ecirc  "&#202;" -- capital E, circumflex accent -->
```

```
<!ENTITY Egrave "&#200;" -- capital E, grave accent -->
<!ENTITY Euml "&#203;" -- capital E, dieresis or umlaut mark-->
<!ENTITY Iacute "&#205;" -- capital I, acute accent -->
<!ENTITY Icirc "&#206;" -- capital I, circumflex accent -->
<!ENTITY Igrave "&#204;" -- capital I, grave accent -->
<!ENTITY Iuml "&#207;" -- capital I, dieresis or umlaut mark-->
<!ENTITY Ntilde "&#209;" -- capital N, tilde -->
<!ENTITY Oacute "&#211;" -- capital O, acute accent -->
<!ENTITY Ocirc "&#212;" -- capital O, circumflex accent -->
<!ENTITY Ograve "&#210;" -- capital O, grave accent -->
<!ENTITY Oslash "&#216;" -- capital O, slash -->
<!ENTITY Otilde "&#213;" -- capital O, tilde -->
<!ENTITY Ouml "&#214;" -- capital O, dieresis or umlaut mark-->
<!ENTITY THORN "&#222;" -- capital THORN, Icelandic -->
<!ENTITY Uacute "&#218;" -- capital U, acute accent -->
<!ENTITY Ucirc "&#219;" -- capital U, circumflex accent -->
<!ENTITY Ugrave "&#217;" -- capital U, grave accent -->
<!ENTITY Uuml "&#220;" -- capital U, dieresis or umlaut mark-->
<!ENTITY Yacute "&#221;" -- capital Y, acute accent -->
<!ENTITY aacute "&#225;" -- small a, acute accent -->
<!ENTITY acirc "&#226;" -- small a, circumflex accent -->
<!ENTITY aelig "&#230;" -- small ae diphthong (ligature) -->
<!ENTITY agrave "&#224;" -- small a, grave accent -->
<!ENTITY amp "&#38;" -- ampersand -->
<!ENTITY aring "&#229;" -- small a, ring -->
<!ENTITY atilde "&#227;" -- small a, tilde -->
<!ENTITY auml "&#228;" -- small a, dieresis or umlaut mark -->
<!ENTITY ccedil "&#231;" -- small c, cedilla -->
<!ENTITY eacute "&#233;" -- small e, acute accent -->
<!ENTITY ecirc "&#234;" -- small e, circumflex accent -->
<!ENTITY egrave "&#232;" -- small e, grave accent -->
<!ENTITY eth "&#240;" -- small eth, Icelandic -->
<!ENTITY euml "&#235;" -- small e, dieresis or umlaut mark -->
<!ENTITY gt "&#62;" -- greater than -->
<!ENTITY iacute "&#237;" -- small i, acute accent -->
<!ENTITY icirc "&#238;" -- small i, circumflex accent -->
<!ENTITY igrave "&#236;" -- small i, grave accent -->
<!ENTITY iuml "&#239;" -- small i, dieresis or umlaut mark -->
<!ENTITY lt "&#60;" -- less than -->
<!ENTITY nbsp "&#32;" -- should be NON_BREAKING space -->
<!ENTITY ntilde "&#241;" -- small n, tilde -->
<!ENTITY oacute "&#243;" -- small o, acute accent -->
<!ENTITY ocirc "&#244;" -- small o, circumflex accent -->
<!ENTITY ograve "&#242;" -- small o, grave accent -->
```

```
<!ENTITY oslash "&#248;" -- small o, slash -->
<!ENTITY otilde "&#245;" -- small o, tilde -->
<!ENTITY ouml "&#246;"  -- small o, dieresis or umlaut mark -->
<!ENTITY szlig "&#223;"-- small sharp s, German (sz ligature)  -->
<!ENTITY thorn "&#254;" -- small thorn, Icelandic -->
<!ENTITY uacute "&#250;" -- small u, acute accent -->
<!ENTITY ucirc "&#251;" -- small u, circumflex accent -->
<!ENTITY ugrave "&#249;" -- small u, grave accent -->
<!ENTITY uuml "&#252;"  -- small u, dieresis or umlaut mark -->
<!ENTITY yacute "&#253;" -- small y, acute accent -->
<!ENTITY yuml "&#255;"  -- small y, dieresis or umlaut mark -->

<!-- deprecated elements -->

<!ELEMENT (%literal) - - CDATA>

<!ELEMENT PLAINTEXT - O EMPTY>
<!-- Local Variables: -->
<!-- mode: sgml -->
<!-- compile-command: "sgmls -s -p " -->
<!-- end: -->
]>
```

Appendix B
Uniform resource locators (URLs)

Location

The topic of *location* is a thorny bush of concepts: To find a resource in the WWW we need a handle of some kind:

- A name distinguishes one object in a distributed system from another.
- The address tells us where it is.
- The route is how to get from here to there.

So a URL tells us where a resource is located. The WWW clients can use to this to reach the correct web server, and the correct page in that server, simply by passing the relevant parts of the URL to the relevant processes and protocols, which then use their routing tables to reach the right place. The authors of URLs call them a *Unifying syntax for the expression of names and addresses of objects on the network*.

Links in Web pages have so far largely been URLs (uniform resource locators). Ideally, they would be "pure" names, since then we could have replication of WWW entries across multiple servers (or mobile information) without having to change the references.

In fact, a URL is a slightly lower level still, and the generic name (whatever generic means) is a universal resource identifier (URI), which sits half way between the idea of a name, and the idea of a locator. An identifier is a unique handle, but does not tell you "what a thing is" or "where it is".

A name allows a user, with the help of a "client" program, to retrieve or operate on objects via a "server" program. A name may be passed for example:

- File Transfer Protocol:
  Host name or IP-address
  [TCP port]
  [user name, password]
  Filename

- WAIS
  Host name or IP-address
  [TCP port]
  local document id

- Gopher
  Host name or IP-address
  [TCP port]
  database name
  selector string

- HTTP
  Host name or IP-address
  [TCP port]
  localobject id

- NNTP
  group Group name
  NNTP article
  Host name
  unique message identifier

- Prospero links
  Host name or IP address
  [UDP port]
  Host specific object name
  [version]
  [identifier]*

- X.500 distinguished name
  Country
  Organization
  Organizational unit
  Person
  Local object identifier

The following sections describes all the commonly used URL prefixes currently in use.

HTTP

The protocol HTTP specifies that the path is handled transparently by those who handle URLs, except for the servers that dereference them. The path is passed by the client to the server with any request, but is not otherwise understood by the client. The fragmentid part is not sent with the request. The search part, if present, is sent. Spaces in URLs should be escaped for transmission in HTTP.

FTP

The ftp: prefix in a URL indicates a file that is to be picked up from the file system of the given host. The protocol FTP is used. The port number, if given, gives the port of the FTP server if not the FTP default. (A client may in practice use local file access to retrieve objects that are available though more efficient means such as local file open or NFS mounting, where this is available and equivalent.)

The syntax allows for the inclusion of a user name and even a password for those systems that do not use the anonymous FTP convention. The default, however, if no user or password is supplied, will be to use that convention, namely that the user name is "anonymous" and the password the user's mail address.

The adoption of a Unix-style syntax involves the conversion into non-Unix local forms by either the client or server. Some non-Unix servers do this, but clients wishing to access sites that do not have Unix-style naming will need certain algorithms to enable other file systems to be identified and treated. Client software may also have to be flexible in terms of the sequence of FTP commands used with different varieties of server. In view of a tendency for file systems to look increasingly similar, it was felt that the URL convention should not be weighed down by extra mechanisms for identifying these cases.

The data format of a file can only, in the general FTP case, be deduced from the name, normally the suffix of the name. This is not standardized. An alternative is for it to be transferred in information outside the URL. The transfer mode (binary or text) must in turn be deduced from the data format. It is recommended that conventions for suffixes of public archives be established, but that is outside the scope of this book.

News

The news locators refer to either news group names or article message identifiers that must conform to the rules of RFC 850. A message identifier may be distinguished from a news group name by the presence of the "@" (commercial at) character. These rules imply that within an article, a reference to a news group or to another article will be a valid URL (in the partial form). Note the following:

- Among URLs, the news: URLs are anomalous in that they are location-independent. They are unsuitable as URN candidates because the NNTP

(Network News Transfer Protocol) architecture relies on the expiry of articles and therefore a small number of articles being available at any one time. When a news: URL is quoted, the assumption is that the reader will fetch the article or group from his or her local news host. News host names are *not* part of news URLs.

- An outstanding problem is that the message identifier is insufficient to allow the retrieval of an expired article, as no algorithm exists for deriving an archive site and file name. The addition of the date and news group set to the article's URL would allow this if a directory existed of archive sites by news group. A further possible extension may be to allow the naming of subject threads as addressable objects.

WAIS

The current WAIS public domain implementation requires that a client know the "type" and length of an object prior to retrieval. These values are returned along with the internal object identifier in the search response. They have been encoded into the path part of the URL in order to make the URL sufficient for the retrieval of the object. If changes to WAIS specifications make the internal id something that is sufficient for later retrieval, then this will not be necessary. Within the WAIS world, names do not of course not need to be prefixed by wais: (by the partial form rules). Although the length is now not strictly necessary, it is kept for historical reasons.

Prospero

The Prospero directory service is used to resolve the URL, yielding an access method for the object (that can then itself be represented as a URL if translated). The host part contains a host name or Internet address. The port part is optional. The path part contains a host specific object name, an optional version number, and an optional list of attributes. If these latter fields are present, they are separated from the host specific object name and from each other by the characters %00 (per cent, zero, zero), this being an escaped string terminator (null). If the optional list of attributes is provided, the version number must be present, but may be the empty string (i.e. the first attribute would be separated from the host specific name by %00%00). External Prospero links are represented directly as URLs of the underlying access method and are not represented as Prospero URLs.

Gopher

The first character of the URL path part (after the initial single slash) is a single-character type field, which is that used by the Gopher protocol. The rest of the path is the "selector string", with disallowed characters encoded. Note that some selector strings begin with a copy of the Gopher type character, in which case that character will occur twice consecutively in the URL. If the type character and selector are omitted, the type defaults to "1". Gopher links that refer to non-Gopher protocols are represented directly as URLs of the underlying access method and are not represented as Gopher URLs.

Telnet, Rlogin, TN3270

The use of URLs to represent interactive sessions is a convenient extension to their uses for objects. This allows access to information systems that only provide an interactive service and no information server. As information within the service cannot be addressed individually or, in general, automatically retrieved, this is a less desirable, though currently common, solution.

X.500

The mapping of X.500 names onto URLs is not defined here. A decision is required as to whether "distinguished names" or "user friendly names" (ufn), or both, should be allowed. If any punctuation conversions are needed from the adopted X.500 representation (such as the use of slashes between parts of a ufn), they must be defined. This is a subject for study.

Whois

This prefix describes the access using the "whois++" scheme. The hostname part is the same as for other IP-based schemes. The path part can be either a whois handle for a whois object, or it can be a valid whois query string. This is a subject for further study.

Network management database

This had not been defined at the time of writing.

Registration of naming schemes

A new naming scheme may be introduced by defining a mapping onto a conforming URL syntax, using a new scheme identifier. Experimental scheme identifiers may be used by mutual agreement between parties, and must start with the characters "x-". The scheme name urn: is reserved for the work in progress on a scheme for more persistent names. Therefore URNs (names) and URLs (locators) will be indistinguishable. An object that is either a URL or a URN is known as a URI (Identifier).

It is proposed that the Internet Assigned Numbers Authority (IANA) perform the function of registration of new schemes. Any submission of a new URI scheme must include a definition of an algorithm for the retrieval of any object within that scheme. The algorithm must take the URI and produce either a set of URL(s) that will lead to the desired object or the object itself, in a well-defined or determinable format.

It is recommended that those proposing a new scheme demonstrate its utility and operability by the provision of a gateway that will provide images of objects in the new scheme for clients using an existing protocol. If the new scheme is not a locator scheme, then the properties of names in the new space should be clearly defined. It is likewise recommended that, where a protocol allows for retrieval by URI, the client software has provision for being configured to use specific gateway locators for indirect access through new naming schemes.

Uniform resource locator (URL) grammar

BNF syntax

The following is a BNF-like description of the uniform resource locator syntax. A vertical line "|" indicates alternatives, and [brackets] indicate optional parts. Spaces are represented by the word "space", and the vertical line character by "vline". Single letters stand for single letters. All words of more than one letter are entities described somewhere in this description. The "generic" production gives a higher level parsing of the same URLs as the other productions. The "national" and "punctuation" characters do not appear in any productions and therefore may not appear in URLs. The afsaddress is left in as an historical note, but is not a url production.

```
fragmentaddress   uri [ # fragmentid ]
uri               url
url               generic | httpaddress | ftpaddress |
                  newsaddress | prosperoaddress | telnetaddress
```

	| gopheraddress | waisaddress
generic	scheme : path [? search]
scheme	ialpha
httpaddress	h t t p : / / hostport [/ path] [? search]
ftpaddress	f t p : / / login / path
afsaddress	a f s : / / cellname / path
newsaddress	n e w s : groupart
waisaddress	waisindex | waisdoc
waisindex	w a i s : / / hostport / database [? search]
waisdoc	w a i s : / / hostport / database / wtype / digits / path
groupart	* | group | article
group	ialpha [. group]
article	xalphas @ host
database	xalphas
wtype	xalphas
prosperoaddress	prosperolink
prosperolink	p r o s p e r o : / / hostport / hsoname [% 0 0 version [attributes]]
hsoname	path
version	digits
attributes	attribute [attributes]
attribute	alphanums
telnetaddress	t e l n e t : / / login
gopheraddress	g o p h e r : / / hostport [/ gtype [selector]] [? search]
login	[user [: password] @] hostport
hostport	host [: port]
host	hostname | hostnumber
cellname	hostname
hostname	ialpha [. hostname]
hostnumber	digits . digits . digits . digits
port	digits
selector	path
path	void | xpalphas [/ path]
search	xalphas [+ search]
user	xalphas
password	xalphas
fragmentid	xalphas
gtype	xalpha
xalpha	alpha | digit | safe | extra | escape
xalphas	xalpha [xalphas]
xpalpha	xalpha | +
xpalphas	xpalpha [xpalpha]
ialpha	alpha [xalphas]

alpha	a | b | c | d | e | f | g | h | i | j | k |
	l | m | n | o | p | q | r | s | t | u | v |
	w | x | y | z | A | B | C | D | E | F | G |
	H | I | J | K | L | M | N | O | P | Q | R |
	S | T | U | V | W | X | Y | Z
digit	0 |1 | 2 | 3 | 4 | 5 | 6 | 7 | 8 | 9
safe	$ | - | _ | @ | . | &
extra	! | * | " | ' | (|) | : | ; | . | space
escape	% hex hex
hex	digit | a | b | c | d | e | f | A | B | C |
	D | E | F
national	{ | } | vline | [|] | \ | ^ | ~
punctuation	< | >
digits	digit [digits]
alphanum	alpha | digit
alphanums	alphanum [alphanums]
void	

Wrappers for URIs in plain text

URIs, including URLs, will ideally be transmitted though protocols that accept them and data formats that define a context for them. However, in practice nowadays, there are many occasions when URLs are included in plain ASCII non-marked-up text such as electronic mail and usenet news messages.

In this case, it is convenient to have a separate wrapper syntax to define delimiters that will enable the human or automated reader to recognize that the URI is a URI. The recommendation is that the angle brackets (less than and greater than signs) of the ASCII set be used for this purpose. These wrappers do not form part of the URL, are not mandatory and should not be used in contexts (such as SGML parameters, HTTP requests, etc.) in which delimiters are already specified. An example is:

```
Yes, Jim, I found it under <ftp://info.cern.ch/pub> but you can
probably pick it up from <ftp://ds.internic.net/rfc>.
```

Security considerations

The URL scheme does not in itself pose a security threat. Users should beware that there is no general guarantee that a URL that points to a given object at any one time will continue to do so. Indeed, at some later time it may even point to a different object as a result of the movement of objects on servers.

The use of URLs containing passwords is clearly unwise.

Appendix C
Hypertext Transfer Protocol (HTTP)

A stateless search, retrieve and manipulation protocol

The protocol is basically stateless. It is a transaction consisting of:

- *connection* the establishment of a connection by the client to the server; when TCP/IP is used, port 80 is the well-known port, but other non-reserved ports may be specified in the URL;
- *request* the sending, by the client, of a request message to the server;
- *response* the sending, by the server, of a response to the client;
- *close* the closing of the connection by either or both parties.

The HTTP protocol

Request

The request is sent with a first line containing the method to be applied to the object requested, the identifier of the object, and the protocol version in use, followed by further information encoded in the RFC 822 header style. The format of the request is:

```
Request                =    SimpleRequest | FullRequest
SimpleRequest          =    GET <uri> CrLf
FullRequest            =    Method UR ProtocolVersion CrLf
                            [*<HTRQ Header>]
                            [<CrLf> <data>]
<Method>               =    <InitialAlpha>
ProtocolVersion        =    HTTP/V1.0
uri                    =    <as defined in URL spec>
<HTRQ Header>          =    <Fieldname> : <Value> <CrLf>
```

```
<data>              =   MIME-conforming-message
```

The URI is the uniform resource locator (URL) as defined in the specification or may be (when it is defined) a uniform resource name (URN), when a specification for this is settled, for servers that support URN resolution.

Unless the server is being used as a gateway, a partial URL shall be given with the assumptions of the protocol (http:) and server (the server that provided the current document) being obvious.

The URI should be encoded using the escaping scheme described in the URL specification to a level such that (at least) spaces and control characters (decimal 0–31 and 128–159) do not appear unescaped.

Note: The rest of an HTTP URL after the host name and optional port number is completely opaque to the client; the client may make no deductions about the object from its URL.

Protocol version

The Protocol/Version field defines the format of the rest of the request. At the moment only HTTP/1.0 is in use. If the protocol version is not specified, the server assumes that the browser uses HTTP version 0.9.

Uniform resource identifier (URI)

This is a string identifying the object. It contains no blanks. It maybe a uniform resource locator (URL) defining the address of an object, or it may be a representation of the name of an object (URN, universal resource name), where that object has been registered in some name space. At the time of writing, no suitable naming system exists, but this protocol will accept such names so long as they are distinguishable from the existing URL name spaces.

Request headers

These are RFC 822 format headers with special field names given in the list below, as well as any other HTTP object headers or MIME headers.

Object body

The content of an object is sent (depending on the method) with the request and/or the reply.

Methods

The Method field in HTTP indicates the method to be performed on the object identified by the URL. The method GET below is always supported.

This list may be extended from time to time by a process of registration with the design authority. Method names are case sensitive. Currently specified methods are as follows:

- GET means retrieve whatever data is identified by the URI, so where the URI refers to a data-producing process, or a script that can be run by such a process, it is this data that will be returned and not the source text of the script or process. Also used for searches.

- HEAD is the same as GET but returns only HTTP headers and no document body.

- CHECKOUT is similar to GET but locks the object against update by other people. The lock may be broken by a higher authority or on timeout: in this case a future CHECKIN will fail.

- SHOWMETHOD returns a description (perhaps a form) for a given method when applied to the given object. The method name is specified in a For-Method: field.

- PUT specifies that the data in the body section are to be stored under the supplied URL. The URL must already exist. The new contents of the document are the data part of the request. POST and REPLY should be used for creating new documents.

- DELETE requests that the server delete the information corresponding to the given URL. After a successful DELETE method, the URL becomes invalid for any future methods.

- POST creates a new object linked to the specified object. The message-id field of the new object maybe set by the client or else will be given by the server. A URL will be allocated by the server and returned to the client. The new document is the data part of the request. It is considered to be subordinate to the specified object, in the way that a file is subordinate to a directory containing it, or a news article is subordinate to a newsgroup to which it is posted.

- LINK links an existing object to the specified object.

- UNLINK removes link (or other meta-) information from an object.

- CHECKIN is similar to PUT, but releases the lock set on the object. It fails if no lock has been set by CHECKOUT.

- TEXTSEARCH; the object may be queried with a text string. The search form of the GET method is used to query the object.

- SPACEJUMP; the object will accept a query whose terms are the co-ordinates of a point within the object. The method is implemented using GET with a derived URL.

- SEARCH (proposed only); the index (etc.) identified by the URL is to be searched for something matching in some sense the enclosed message. How does the client know what message formats are acceptable to the server?

Response

The response from the server shall start with the following syntax (see also note on client tolerance):

```
<status line>  ::=  <HTTP version> <status code> <reason line>
<CrLf>
<HTTP version> ::=  3*<digit>
<status code>  ::=  3*<digit>
<digit>        ::=  0 | 1 | 2 | 3 | 4 | 5 | 6 | 7 | 8 | 9
<reason line> ::=  * <printable>
```

- `<HTTP version>` identifies the HyperText Transfer Protocol version being used by the server. For the version described by this document it is `HTTP/1.0`.
- `<status code>` gives the coded results of the attempt to understand and satisfy the request. A three-digit ASCII decimal number.
- `<reason string>` gives an explanation for a human reader, except where noted for particular status codes.

Fields on the status line are delimited by a single blank (parsers should accept any amount of white space). The possible values of the status code are listed below.

Response headers

The headers include RFC 822 format, as well as any MIME conforming headers, notably the content type field.

Response data

Additional information may follow, in the format of a MIME message body. The significance of the data depends on the status code. The content-type used for the data may be any content type that the client has expressed his ability to accept, or text/plain, or text/html. That is, one can always assume that the client can handle text/plain and text/html.

Status codes

The values of the numeric status code to HTTP requests are as follows. The data sections of messages Error, Forward and Redirection responses may be used to contain human-readable diagnostic information.

Success 2xx

These codes indicate success. The body section, if present, is the object returned by the request. It is a MIME format object. It is in MIME format and may only be in text/plain, text/html or one of the formats specified as acceptable in the request.

- OK 200   The request was fulfilled.
- CREATED 201   Following a POST command, this indicates success, but the textual part of the response line indicates the URI by which the newly created document should be known.
- Accepted 202   The request has been accepted for processing, but the processing has not been completed. The request may or may not eventually be acted upon, as it may be disallowed when processing actually takes place. There is no facility for status returns from asynchronous operations such as this.
- Partial Information 203   When received in the response to a GET command, this indicates that the returned meta-information is not a definitive set of the object from a server with a copy of the object, but is from a private overlaid web. This may include annotation information about the object, for example

Error 4xx, 5xx

The 4xx codes are intended for cases in which the client seems to have erred, and the 5xx codes for the cases in which the server is aware that the server has erred. It is impossible to distinguish these cases in general, so the difference is only informational. The body section may contain a document describing the error in human readable form. The document is in MIME format, and may only be in text/plain, text/html or one for the formats specified as acceptable in the request.

- Bad Request 400   The request had bad syntax or was inherently impossible to be satisfied.
- Unauthorized 401   The parameter to this message gives a specification of authorization schemes that are acceptable. The client should retry the request with a suitable Authorization header.
- Payment Required 402   The parameter to this message gives a specification of charging schemes acceptable. The client may retry the request

with a suitable ChargeTo header.

- Forbidden 403   The request is for something forbidden. Authorization will not help.
- Not Found 404   The server has not found anything matching the URI given.
- Internal Error 500   The server encountered an unexpected condition that prevented it from fulfilling the request.
- Not Implemented 501   The server does not support the facility required.

Redirection 3xx

The codes in this section indicate action to be taken (normally automatically) by the client in order to fulfil the request.

- Moved 301   The data requested has been assigned a new URI, the change is permanent. (Note that this is an optimization, which must, pragmatically, be included in this definition. Browsers with link-editing capability should automatically relink to the new reference, where possible.) The response contains one or more header lines of the form

  Location: *URL*

  or

  URI: *<URI>*

  that specify alternative addresses for the object in question. URI is the later form and will replace Location. Some servers may give both lines in one response.
- Found 302   The data requested actually resides under a different URL. However, the redirection may be altered on occasion (when making links to these kinds of document, the browser should default to using the Udi of the redirection document, but have the option of linking to the final document) as for Forward. The response format is the same as for Moved.
- Method 303

  Method:*method URL*
  body-section

  Like the found response, this suggests that the client go try another network address. In this case, a different method may be used too, rather than GET. The body-section contains the parameters to be used for the method. This allows a document to be a pointer to a complex query operation.

Appendix D
Multipurpose Internet Mail Extensions (MIME)

This appendix contains the complete Extended BNF grammar for all the syntax specified in the MIME standard.

By itself, however, this grammar is incomplete. It refers to several entities that are defined by RFC 822. Rather than reproduce those definitions here, and risk unintentional differences between the two, this document simply refers the reader to RFC 822 for the remaining definitions. Wherever a term is undefined, it refers to the RFC 822 definition.

```
application-subtype := ("octet-stream" *stream-param) / "postscript" /
                       extension-token

application-type := "application" "/" application-subtype

attribute := token  ; case-insensitive

atype := "ftp" / "anon-ftp" / "tftp" / "local-file"/ "afs" /
                "mail-server" / extension-token; Case-insensitive

audio-type := "audio" "/" ("basic" / extension-token)

body-part := <"message" as defined in RFC 822, with all header fields
             optional, and with the specified delimiter not occurring
             anywhere in the message body, either on a line by itself
             or as a substring anywhere.>
```

NOTE: In certain transport enclaves, RFC 822 restrictions such as the one that limits bodies to printable ASCII characters may not be in force. (That is, the transport domains may resemble standard Internet mail transport as specified in RFC821 and assumed by RFC822, but without certain restrictions.) The relaxation of these restrictions should be construed as locally extending the definition of bodies, for example to include octets outside of the ASCII range, as long as these extensions are supported by the transport and adequately documented in the Content-Transfer-Encoding header field. However, in no event are headers (either message headers or body-part headers) allowed to contain anything other than ASCII characters.

boundary := 0*69<bchars> bcharsnospace

bchars := bcharsnospace / " "

bcharsnospace := DIGIT / ALPHA / "'" / "(" / ")" / "+" / "_"/ "." / "-" /
                 "." / "/" / ":" / "=" / "?"

charset := "us-ascii" / "iso-8859-1" / "iso-8859-2"/ "iso-8859-3"
           / "iso-8859-4" / "iso-8859-5" / "iso-8859-6"
           / "iso-8859-7"/ "iso-8859-8" / "iso-8859-9"
           / extension-token; case insensitive

close-delimiter := "—" boundary "—" CRLF;Again,no space by "—".

content := "Content-Type" ":" type "/" subtype *(";" parameter)
           ; case-insensitive matching of type and subtype

delimiter := "—" boundary CRLF ;taken from Content-Type field.
             ; There must be no space
             ; between "—" and boundary.

description := "Content-Description" ":" *text

discard-text := *(*text CRLF)

encapsulation := delimiter body-part CRLF

encoding := "Content-Transfer-Encoding" ":" mechanism

epilogue := discard-text   ; to be ignored upon receipt.

extension-token := x-token / iana-token

external-param := (";" "access-type" "=" atype)
                  / (";" "expiration" "=" date-time)
                  ; Note that date-time is quoted / (";" "size" "="
                  1*DIGIT) / (";" "permission" "=" ("read"
                  / "read-write"))
                  ; Permission is case-insensitive
                  / (";" "name" "=" value)
                  / (";" "site" "=" value)
                  / (";" "dir" "=" value)
                  / (";" "mode" "=" value)
                  / (";" "server" "=" value)
                  / (";" "subject" "=" value)
     ;access-type required; others required based on access-type

```
iana-token := <a publicly-defined extension token,registered with IANA, as
               specified in appendix E>

id := "Content-ID" ":" msg-id

image-type := "image" "/" ("gif" / "jpeg" / extension-token)

mechanism :=   "7bit"  ; case-insensitive
             / "quoted-printable"
             / "base64"
             / "8bit"
             / "binary"
             / x-token

message-subtype := "rfc822"
                 / "partial" 2#3partial-param
                 / "external-body" 1*external-param
                 / extension-token

message-type := "message" "/" message-subtype

multipart-body :=preamble 1*encapsulation close-delimiter epilogue

multipart-subtype := "mixed" / "parallel" / "digest"
                   / "alternative" / extension-token

multipart-type := "multipart" "/" multipart-subtype
                  ":" "boundary" "=" boundary

octet := "=" 2(DIGIT / "A" / "B" / "C" / "D" / "E" / "F")
                 ; octet must be used for characters > 127, =, SPACE, or TAB,
                 ; and is recommended for any characters not listed in
                 ; Appendix B as "mail-safe".

padding := "0" / "1" / "2" / "3" / "4" / "5" / "6" / "7"

parameter := attribute "=" value

partial-param :=   (";" "id" "=" value)
                 / (";" "number" "=" 1*DIGIT)
                 / (";" "total" "=" 1*DIGIT)
                 ; id & number required;total required for last part

preamble := discard-text    ; to be ignored upon receipt.

ptext := octet / <any ASCII character except "=", SPACE, or TAB>
                 ; characters not listed as "mail-safe" in Appendix B
                 ; are also not recommended.

quoted-printable := ([*(ptext / SPACE / TAB) ptext] ["="] CRLF)
                 ; Maximum line length of 76 characters excluding CRLF
```

```
stream-param := (":" "type" "=" value)
               / (":" "padding" "=" padding)

subtype := token ; case-insensitive

text-subtype := "plain" / extension-token

text-type := "text" "/" text-subtype [":" "charset" "=" charset]

token := 1*<any (ASCII) CHAR except SPACE, CTLs, or tspecials>

tspecials := "(" / ")" / "<" / ">" / "@"/ "," / ";" / ":" / "\" / <">/ "/"
             / "[" / "]" / "?" / "="
             ; Must be in quoted-string,
             ; to use within parameter values

type :=   "application"  / "audio"  ; case-insensitive
             / "image"       / "message"
             / "multipart" / "text"
             / "video"       / extension-token
             ; All values case-insensitive

value := token / quoted-string

version := "MIME-Version" ":" 1*DIGIT "." 1*DIGIT

video-type := "video" "/" ("mpeg" / extension-token)

x-token := <The two characters "X-" or "x-" followed, with no intervening
             white space, by any token>
```

Sources

Who or what are RFCs?

RFCs are request for comments. This is a series of documents about the Internet and its protocols, maintained by the RFC editor, who is appointed by the Internet Advisory Board (IAB), who are selected/voted for by the Internet Society.

Some RFCs specify Internet standards, developed (usually) by the IAB's Internet Engineering Task Force, and ratified by the Internet Engineering Steering Group of the IAB. These are listed in the list of standards RFCs.

Appendix E
URLs cited

Home of the Association of Computing Machinery
    http://acm.org/
Virtual architecture
    http://alberti.mit.edu:80/arch/4.207/texts/city-of-bits4.html
http://american.recordings.com/wwwofmusic/ubl.html
Carl Phillips Yachting
    http://beta.aladdin.co.uk/cpy/
http://cbl.leeds.ac.uk/nikos/tex2html/doc/latex2html/latex2html.html
A source of the Internet Assistant
    http://debra.dgbt.doc.ca/ia/ia.html
Dow Vision
    http://dowvision.wais.net:5554/dv.html
A source of Internet information
    http://ds.internic.net/ds/
ARPA Project Information
    http://ftp.arpa.mil/ResearchAreas/NETS/Internet.html
ACM's Computer Communicatons Review
    http://gatekeeper.dec.com/pub/doc/sigcomm/ccr/overview.html
The Bay Area Gigatbit Network
    http://george.lbl.gov/BAGNet.html
Information about Internet economics
    http://gopher.econ.lsa.umich.edu/EconInternet/Pricing.html
Cern WWW pages
    http://info.cern.ch/hypertext/WWW
The Internet Society
    http://info.isoc.org/
Sun's Java language and system
    http://java.sun.com/
A Lego enthusiast's page

http://legowww.itek.norut.no/
The Louvre
http://mistral.enst.fr/~pioch/louvre/
The *New York Times*
http://nytimesfax.com/
The author of Tcl's home page
http://playground.sun.com/~ouster/
The Xerox map
http://pubweb.parc.xerox.com/map
All the UK
http://src.doc.ic.ac.uk/all-uk.html
The complete works of Shakespeare
http://the-tech.mit.edu/Shakespeare/works.html
Something about MPEG
http://w3.eeb.ele.tue.nl/mpeg/index.html
About security
http://web.cnam.fr/Network/Crypto/
About spiders and robots
http://web.nexor.co.uk/mak/doc/robots/norobots.html
About Acrobat
http://www.adobe.com/Software.html#acrosun
A share information feed
http://www.ai.mit.edu/stocks.html
About ATM
http://www.atmforum.com/
A bank
http://www.barclays.co.uk/
BBC
http://www.bbcnc.org.uk/
British Telecommunications plc
http://www.bt.net/
Another TV company
http://www.cityscape.co.uk/channel4/
Future networks
http://www.cnri.reston.va.us:4000/public/gigabit.html
Ourselves
http://www.cs.ucl.ac.uk/
Online books
http://www.demon.co.uk/bookshop/
Online careers
http://www.demon.co.uk/westlake/careerlake.html
A publisher
http://www.elsevier.nl/
A PC network stack company

http://www.ftp.com/
First Virtual Holdings
http://www.fv.com/
Housing
http://www.gems.com/realestate/
Seismology
http://www.geo.mtu.edu:80/volcanoes/rabaul/
Paleantology
http://www.hcc.hawaii.edu/dinos/dinos.1.html
PD software lumber yard
http://www.hensa.ac.uk/
IETF information
http://www.ietf.cnri.reston.va.us/home.html
Internet information
http://www.internic.net:80/newsletter/
Music and films
http://www.iuma.com/Warner/html/artists.html
Bespoke numerical software
http://www.nag.co.uk:70/
NCSA
http://www.ncsa.uiuc.edu
UK Government
http://www.open.gov.uk/
The *Electronic Telegraph*
http://www.telegraph.co.uk/
The *Times*
http://www.timeshigher.newsint.co.uk/
My Alma Mater
http://www.trin.cam.ac.uk/
UK Educational And Research Networks Assoc
http://www.ukerna.ac.uk/
Wired
http://www.wired.com/

Glossary

ACL   access control list. Users with permission to get at a resource

API   application programming interface. Standard programming library for using some facility

ARPANET   Advanced Research Project Agency's Network. The original core of the Internet

ATM   Asynchronous Transfer Mode. A new high speed low level networking technology (also, automatic teller machine – cashpoint)

BinHexed   compressed and encoded for ASCII transmission over a network

BNF   Backus Naur Form – a standard way of expressing the grammar computer languages

CD   compact disc. Non-writable digital storage, laser-readable originally for domestic hi-fi audio market, now also used for software distribution and extended through Philips CD-Interactive to provide more flexible entertainment

CERN   Conseil Européen pour la Recherche Nucléaire – the source of the Web

CGI   Common Gateway Interface. An API between WWW servers and backend programs

DCA   Defense Communications Agency

DIY   do it yourself

DNS   Domain Name System

daemon   a network server program, typically on a Unix system

datagram   unit of transfer at the lowest level of the Internet, also called a packet

Ethernet   the most widespread local area network technology

FTP   File Transfer Protocol. The traditional Internet tool for moving files around interactively

GIF   Graphics Interchange Format.

GUI   graphical user interface, e.g. Mosaic (cf. a command line interface, e.g. DOS)

HTML Hyper Text Markup Language.

HTTP HyperText Transfer Protocol

Hotlist personal list of frequently visited resources in the Web

HyperText human-readable information annotated with structural links between non-sequential sections

IAB Internet Advisory Board. Elected technical board under the Internet Society that advises on standards.

IANA Internet Assigned Number Authority. Gives out protocol and system identifiers

IETF Internet Engineering Task Force. Does the work to develop Internet Systems and Standards

IP Internet Protocol. Currently version 4

IP6 the next generation Internet Protocol

ISBN International Standard Book Number

ISDN Integrated Services Digital Network. Digital telephone lines

ISO International Standards Organization

ITU International Telecommunications Union. Sets standards for public network operators ("telcos")

JPEG Joint Picture Expert Group. ISO group that developed the still-picture compression standard encoding commonly known as JPEG

KA9Q ham radio call sign of Phil Karn, and software for PCs to Internetwork.

Kerberos authentication system from MIT

LAN local area network. A network in a single building or office, e.g. an Ethernet.

MIME Multipurpose Internet Mail Extensions

MPEG Motion Picture Expert Group. Compressed digital TV standards group in ISO. MPEG I and MPEG II are standards commonly used to store and transfer video.

Mbone Multicast Backbone. The part of the Internet capable of interactive video and audio between multiple simultaneous participants

MUDs Multiuser Dungeons

NCSA National Center for Superconducting Applications, at the University of Illinois at Urbana-Champagne – a source of Web software

NIC Network Information Centre

NNTP Network News Transfer Protocol

NSA National Security Agency. US Government Agency that deals with Cryptosystems

NSFNet National Science Foundation's Network. Originally the US Academic and Research portion of the Internet

PGP (Pretty Good Privacy) a public domain package for extremely good authentication and encryption of messages

Perl a programming language for rapid development of tools.

RDP Reliable Data Protocol – something built on UDP to provide reliability and message exchanging

RPC   Remote Procedure Call

SGML   Standard Generalized Markup Language. ISO standard upon which HTML rests.

SMTP   Simple Mail Transfer Protocol

TCL   Tool Command Language. Another programming system, like Perl

UDP   User Datagram Protocol – the simplest of the Internet's transport protocols

URI   universal resource indicator

URL   uniform resource locator

URN   universal resource name

Index